Mastering n8n

The No-Code Automation Guide to Workflow
Automation with 350+ Integrations

Hawke Nexon

Table of content

Foreword

A.1 A Note from the Author

Welcome to **"Mastering n8n: The No-Code Automation Guide to Workflow Automation with 350+ Integrations"**! Whether you're just starting your journey with workflow automation or you're an experienced professional looking to enhance your skills, this book is designed to be your comprehensive guide. I've written this book to provide practical, hands-on guidance to anyone interested in automating their workflows using the powerful n8n platform.

In the pages that follow, you will find not only the core concepts of n8n, but also detailed instructions, flowcharts, and tables to help break down complex processes and give you actionable steps to build real-world automation workflows. I've crafted this book to be approachable for both beginners and seasoned users, ensuring that you can find value at any stage of your automation journey.

Thank you for choosing this book. I hope it serves as both a learning tool and a reference guide as you dive into the world of automation with n8n.

A.2 Why I Wrote This Book

When I first encountered n8n, I was struck by its potential to revolutionize how businesses and individuals approach automation. Unlike many other automation platforms that require extensive coding knowledge, n8n offers an intuitive no-code environment that empowers users to create complex workflows with ease. This flexibility, coupled with the vast range of integrations, made n8n stand out as the go-to solution for anyone looking to automate processes across a wide array of services and applications.

However, I noticed that despite its power, there was a lack of detailed resources that could guide users from beginner to expert in a structured and practical manner. This gap in accessible, actionable content is what motivated me to write this book. Through this guide, I aim to provide clear, step-by-step instructions and well-organized explanations so that you can harness the full potential of n8n for your own workflow automation needs.

Automation is no longer a luxury or a complex technical task—it's a necessity in today's fast-paced digital world. With n8n, it's possible to automate tasks efficiently, saving time, reducing errors, and increasing productivity. It's my goal to ensure that by the time you reach the last chapter, you will not only be proficient in using n8n but also equipped to build powerful workflows that serve your specific needs.

A.3 Who This Book Is For

This book is designed for a wide range of readers—from complete beginners who are just starting to explore automation to more experienced users who want to deepen their knowledge and leverage the full potential of n8n's capabilities.

Here's a breakdown of who will benefit the most from this book:

- **Beginners in Workflow Automation**: If you're new to workflow automation and have little or no experience with no-code platforms, this book will guide you step by step. I'll introduce key concepts in a clear and simple manner, making it easy to get started with n8n. By the end of the book, you will be comfortable building your own workflows to automate repetitive tasks.

- **Small Business Owners & Entrepreneurs**: If you're looking to save time and improve efficiency in your business processes, this book is perfect for you. You don't need to be a programmer to set up automations in n8n. Whether it's automating email notifications, syncing customer data, or managing leads, n8n can help you streamline your operations without needing to rely on external developers.

- **Developers & Technical Users**: If you're a developer or have some technical experience, you'll appreciate the more advanced techniques covered in this book. I'll show you how to customize nodes, write functions, and integrate n8n with APIs and webhooks, enabling you to tackle complex automation challenges that require coding.

- **Teams & Enterprises**: For teams looking to implement automation across different functions, this book provides the tools to build collaborative workflows. From integrating marketing tools to automating project management tasks, n8n's flexibility allows for solutions that scale within teams or enterprises.

- **Automation Enthusiasts & Makers**: If you're passionate about building efficient, automated systems, this book will give you the knowledge to create your own customized solutions using n8n's powerful features. You'll find valuable insights into workflow design, best practices, and integration strategies to help you build advanced automation workflows that suit your unique needs.

Whether you are automating simple tasks or designing complex workflows, this book is structured to meet you wherever you are on your automation journey. You'll gain the skills and confidence to use n8n effectively and apply automation in ways that are both practical and innovative.

Introduction

B.1 What Is n8n?

n8n is an open-source, powerful, and flexible automation platform that allows you to create complex workflows between a wide range of applications and services. The key feature of n8n is its no-code approach, making it accessible to non-technical users while also offering customization options for developers. By using n8n, you can automate repetitive tasks, streamline processes, and integrate different systems without writing extensive code.

At its core, n8n enables users to create workflows—sequences of actions triggered by specific events or conditions. These workflows can integrate various third-party services, APIs, and internal tools, allowing users to automate everything from data syncing to customer notifications.

One of the most notable advantages of n8n is its **extensive library of over 350 integrations** with popular tools like Google Sheets, Slack, GitHub, Trello, and many more. This vast selection makes it easy for users to connect different platforms seamlessly and automate their tasks.

Whether you need to automate simple tasks or design complex business logic, n8n offers a visual interface where users can drag and drop nodes (representing various actions) to build workflows. Advanced users can even extend n8n with custom code or integrate with external APIs to create more sophisticated workflows.

B.2 The Rise of No-Code Automation

In recent years, the demand for workflow automation has skyrocketed. As businesses and individuals continue to look for ways to improve efficiency and reduce repetitive tasks, no-code platforms have emerged as a key solution. No-code automation allows users to create and manage workflows without needing to have programming expertise. This democratization of automation has empowered both technical and non-technical users to take control of their workflows and integrate their tools without waiting for development teams.

The rise of no-code platforms like n8n has played a major role in the movement towards easier, faster, and more accessible automation. Traditional automation solutions often required specialized coding skills or expensive development resources. With the no-code approach, users can achieve automation quickly and cost-effectively, unlocking new levels of productivity for businesses, teams, and individuals alike.

Moreover, as companies become more digitally connected and rely on an ever-growing suite of cloud services, the need for seamless integration between different systems is greater than ever.

No-code automation platforms, like n8n, provide the ability to bridge gaps between various services, creating a connected ecosystem where data flows effortlessly between platforms.

n8n, in particular, stands out for its flexibility, extensibility, and community-driven development. It is not just another tool in the no-code automation landscape but a versatile platform that combines ease of use with powerful features for users across all skill levels. It has become the go-to solution for anyone looking to automate their digital workflows, and it's only growing as more integrations and features are added regularly.

B.3 How This Book Is Structured

This book is designed to take you through a step-by-step journey, starting with the basics and gradually progressing into more advanced concepts. It's structured to cater to readers with varying levels of experience, from beginners to more advanced users, while ensuring practical, real-world applications of n8n automation.

Each chapter is organized into a clear and logical flow, making it easy to understand complex ideas and follow the instructions provided. Here's how each chapter is structured:

1. **Every chapter** begins with a **brief overview**, outlining what you will learn and what the key concepts are.

2. **Learning Objectives**: A concise list of what you will be able to achieve by the end of the chapter. This helps set expectations and gives you a goal to strive toward.

3. **Main Content**: This is where the majority of the learning happens. It's divided into smaller, digestible sections under clearly defined subheadings. These sections often include:

   o **Step-by-step guides**: Instructions on how to achieve specific tasks, presented in a clear, numbered format.

   o **Flowcharts**: Visual representations of processes or decision trees that help explain how workflows work.

   o **Tables**: Structured tables that compare features, methods, or node types.

   o **Code Snippets**: Where applicable, relevant code examples are included to show how to extend n8n's capabilities.

4. **Summary & Recap**: At the end of each chapter, we'll summarize the key points and revisit the learning objectives to ensure you've understood everything. There will also be **discussion questions** or **mini-quizzes** to help reinforce your learning and encourage reflection.

5. **Hands-On Exercises**: To ensure that you can apply what you've learned, each chapter includes practical exercises. These are designed to guide you through the process of building workflows, setting up integrations, or solving common automation problems using n8n.

By the end of the book, you'll have built a strong foundation in using n8n for your automation needs and be equipped to create, optimize, and manage powerful workflows with ease.

B.4 How to Use This Book

This book is designed to be interactive, hands-on, and accessible. Here's how to make the most of it:

1. **Hands-On Learning**: Each chapter contains practical exercises that you should complete as you progress. These exercises are designed to give you real experience in using n8n and reinforce the concepts you've just learned. I encourage you to try the exercises on your own using the n8n platform to ensure you understand how to implement each workflow.

2. **Code Snippets & Downloadable Files**: Throughout the book, you'll find references to code snippets and examples. These are provided to help you build more complex workflows or customize the platform to your needs. For your convenience, downloadable versions of these files (including workflow templates and node configurations) will be available from a dedicated link provided in the book. You can copy and paste these directly into your n8n instance, saving you time and helping you get started quickly.

3. **Access to the n8n Community**: One of the best parts about n8n is its growing community of users and developers. You'll find forums, chat rooms, and online groups where you can share ideas, ask questions, and get advice from other n8n users. As you work through this book, I encourage you to join the **n8n community** to get help, find inspiration, and share your own workflows and automation solutions.

   ○ **Official n8n Community Forum**: The n8n community forum is a great place to ask questions, share workflows, and learn from others.

○ **n8n GitHub Repository**: For those interested in the technical side, the GitHub repository hosts the source code and is a valuable resource for developers looking to contribute or customize n8n.

4. **Using the Online Documentation**: n8n's online documentation is constantly updated and provides in-depth guides and references for every aspect of the platform. As you progress through this book, you may want to consult the official documentation for more detailed information about specific nodes, integrations, or advanced topics.

By combining hands-on exercises, downloadable resources, and access to the vibrant n8n community, this book will give you everything you need to become proficient with n8n and build automation workflows that solve real-world problems.

Chapter 1: Getting Started with n8n

Chapter Objectives

- Install and set up n8n for different environments (Cloud, Desktop, Docker, CLI).
- Explore the n8n User Interface (UI) and its key components.
- Create your first simple workflow and run it.
- Save, test, and debug workflows to ensure they work as expected.
- Understand the Execution Log for troubleshooting and debugging.

1.1 Installing n8n (Cloud, Desktop, Docker, CLI)

Before you can start automating workflows, the first step is to install n8n. This section covers the different methods of installation, so you can choose the one that best fits your environment.

n8n offers a variety of installation options to suit different needs, including cloud-based setups, desktop applications, Docker-based deployments, and installation via the command line interface (CLI). Below is a breakdown of each method:

A. Cloud Installation (n8n Cloud)
If you're looking for a hassle-free solution with no server setup or maintenance required, n8n Cloud is the easiest method. The platform is fully managed, and you can start creating workflows immediately after signing up.

- **Step 1**: Visit n8n.io and sign up for an account.
- **Step 2**: After logging in, click on "Create Workflow."
- **Step 3**: Start building your first workflow directly from the user interface.

Advantages:

- No setup required, everything is managed for you.
- Ideal for beginners who want to focus on automation rather than infrastructure.

Disadvantages:

- Limited to the features available in the cloud version.
- Less control over server performance and configurations.

B. Desktop Installation
For users who prefer running n8n locally, the desktop installation is straightforward and ideal

for personal or small-scale projects. This version runs on your own machine without requiring a cloud server or additional infrastructure.

- **Step 1**: Download the **n8n Desktop App** from the official website.
- **Step 2**: Follow the installation prompts for your operating system (Windows, macOS, or Linux).
- **Step 3**: After installation, open the application and start creating workflows.

Advantages:

- Completely local environment.
- No need for internet connectivity (except for integrations that require APIs).

Disadvantages:

- Not ideal for scalability or collaborative projects.

C. Docker Installation

For users who want more control over the deployment and scalability of n8n, Docker provides a flexible solution. Docker allows you to containerize n8n and deploy it on your local machine or any server.

- **Step 1**: Ensure Docker is installed on your machine.

- **Step 2**: Pull the n8n Docker image using the command:
  docker pull n8nio/n8n

- **Step 3**: Run the n8n container:
  docker run -d --name n8n -p 5678:5678 n8nio/n8n

- **Step 4**: Open your browser and go to http://localhost:5678 to access n8n.

Advantages:

- Easy to scale, deploy on servers, or use in production environments.
- Full control over the environment and customization.

Disadvantages:

- Requires some technical knowledge of Docker.
- Setup can be a bit more complex for beginners.

D. CLI (Command Line Interface) Installation

If you prefer working directly from the command line, you can install n8n using Node.js and npm (Node Package Manager).

- **Step 1**: Ensure you have **Node.js** and **npm** installed.

- **Step 2**: Install n8n globally with the following command:
  npm install n8n -g

- **Step 3**: Start n8n using the command:
  n8n

- **Step 4**: Open http://localhost:5678 in your browser to access the n8n interface.

Advantages:

- Complete control over the environment and dependencies.
- Ideal for developers and users comfortable with the command line.

Disadvantages:

- Requires familiarity with Node.js, npm, and the command line.
- More setup time compared to other methods.

Key Takeaways:

- **Cloud**: Easiest, no setup required.
- **Desktop**: Local, simple, ideal for personal projects.
- **Docker**: Flexible, scalable, and suited for production.
- **CLI**: Developer-friendly, full control, and ideal for advanced users.

1.2 Exploring the User Interface

Once n8n is installed, the next step is to get familiar with its user interface (UI). The n8n UI is intuitive and easy to navigate, designed to help you create, manage, and monitor your workflows.

A. Workflow Area

The Workflow Area is where you will create and edit your workflows. It provides a visual workspace where you can drag and drop nodes to build your automation sequences.

Key Components:

- **Start Node**: Every workflow begins with a trigger node that initiates the process (e.g., when an email arrives).
- **Action Nodes**: These represent the steps that follow the trigger, such as sending an email or making an API call.
- **Connections**: Arrows between nodes show how data flows from one action to the next.

B. Nodes Panel

On the left side of the UI, you'll find the Nodes Panel. This is where you can search and select various nodes to add to your workflow. Nodes are pre-built functions, and there are over 350 available in n8n, ranging from simple actions like sending emails to more advanced tasks like working with databases or APIs.

Key Node Types:

- **Trigger Nodes**: Start your workflow when a specified event occurs (e.g., new tweet, form submission).
- **Action Nodes**: Perform tasks like sending an email, writing to a database, or calling an API.
- **Function Nodes**: Allow you to run custom JavaScript code or manipulate data.

C. Execution Log

The Execution Log, located at the bottom of the screen, provides detailed logs of each workflow execution. It shows the status of every workflow run, including any errors or warnings.

Key Features:

- **Error Messages**: If your workflow fails, the Execution Log will show detailed error messages to help you troubleshoot.
- **Execution History**: You can view past runs and check if your workflow executed successfully.

D. Settings

In the Settings section, you can configure global settings for n8n, including:

- **API Keys**: Manage your credentials for third-party integrations.
- **Server Configuration**: Set up server details if you're running n8n on your own infrastructure.
- **Workflow Sharing**: Options for exporting and sharing workflows.

Key Takeaways:

- **Workflow Area**: The main canvas for creating and editing workflows.
- **Nodes Panel**: A library of nodes that you can drag and drop into your workflows.
- **Execution Log**: Provides feedback on workflow runs, helping with troubleshooting.
- **Settings**: Allows you to manage configurations, integrations, and credentials.

1.3 Creating Your First Workflow

Creating your first workflow is an exciting step! In this section, we'll guide you through building a simple workflow that automates a task. For this example, we'll set up a workflow to automatically send an email when a new row is added to a Google Sheet.

Step 1: Set Up the Trigger Node

The first step in any workflow is to define the trigger — the event that starts the workflow. For this example, we will use a **Google Sheets trigger** that activates the workflow whenever a new row is added.

- **Node Type**: Google Sheets Trigger Node.
- **Configuration**:
    - Authenticate your Google Sheets account by following the prompts.
    - Choose the specific sheet and set the event to trigger whenever a new row is added.

Step 2: Add an Action Node to Send an Email

Once the workflow is triggered, the next action will be to send an email. We'll use the **Send Email** node to configure this step.

- **Node Type**: Email Node (e.g., Gmail, SMTP).
- **Configuration**:
    - Input the email address of the recipient.
    - Set the subject and body of the email, using data from the Google Sheet row (e.g., "New entry added to your sheet: {data from Google Sheet}").

Step 3: Connect the Nodes

To connect the nodes:

- Click on the **Google Sheets Trigger Node**.
- Drag an arrow to the **Send Email Node** to establish the connection.

- The data from the Google Sheets trigger will flow into the email node, allowing you to dynamically populate the email content with the new row's details.

Step 4: Execute the Workflow

Now, it's time to run the workflow and see it in action.

- **Execution**: Click on the "Execute Workflow" button in the top-right corner.
- **Observation**: You should see an email sent to the configured address as soon as a new row is added to the specified Google Sheet.

Key Takeaways:

- You can automate tasks with simple triggers and actions.
- Nodes can be connected in a sequence to define the flow of data.
- n8n workflows allow real-time automation for tasks like sending emails or processing data.

1.4 Saving, Testing, and Debugging

Once you've created a workflow, it's important to save, test, and debug it to ensure it works as expected. This section will help you understand how to do each of these tasks effectively.

Step 1: Saving Your Workflow

To save your workflow:

- **Save Button**: Click the **Save** button located at the top of the screen after you've built your workflow.
- **Naming the Workflow**: A dialog will appear, prompting you to give your workflow a descriptive name (e.g., "Google Sheets to Email").
- **Saving Version**: You can also create multiple versions of your workflow, allowing you to revert to a previous version if needed.

Step 2: Testing Your Workflow

Testing your workflow is an important step before you fully deploy it. You can test workflows in two ways: manually or automatically.

- **Manual Test**: Trigger the workflow by performing the event that should start it (e.g., add a new row to the Google Sheet).

- **Test Button**: You can also use the **Test Workflow** button to simulate the trigger without waiting for the real event.

Important Consideration:

- Ensure that your nodes are properly configured, especially authentication and input/output data fields, before testing.

Step 3: Debugging Your Workflow

Debugging is crucial to fixing errors in your workflow. n8n provides several ways to troubleshoot and debug workflows:

- **Execution Log**: Check the **Execution Log** for any errors during the workflow run. If a step fails, the log will provide detailed error messages to help you identify the issue.
  Example Error: "Failed to connect to Google Sheets – Invalid credentials."
  Action: Reconfigure the Google Sheets authentication node.
- **Highlight Errors in the Workflow**: If a node fails, it will be marked with a red icon. Clicking on this node will show you additional details, such as error messages and failed executions.
- **Pause the Workflow for Debugging**: If you're unsure where the workflow is failing, you can use the **Pause** option in a node to stop the execution after a certain point. This allows you to inspect the data flow before proceeding.

Step 4: Rerun the Workflow

After fixing any errors, you can rerun the workflow from the beginning to ensure that it functions correctly.

- **Rerun from Last Successful Execution**: In the Execution Log, you can choose to rerun the workflow from the last successful execution point.
- **Full Execution**: You can choose to run the entire workflow again from the start to confirm that everything works as intended.

Key Takeaways:

- Always save your workflows to prevent losing progress.
- Test workflows manually and automatically to ensure functionality.
- Use the Execution Log and error markers to help debug and fix issues quickly.

1.5 Understanding the Execution Log

After a workflow is executed in n8n—whether manually or automatically—it is essential to review how it performed. The **Execution Log** is n8n's built-in tool for visualizing, tracking, and debugging workflow executions. Understanding it will help you optimize and troubleshoot your automations with precision.

Learning Objectives

By the end of this section, you will be able to:

- Navigate and interpret the Execution Log interface.
- Diagnose errors and performance issues.
- Analyze node input/output data for debugging.
- Use execution history to rerun or improve workflows.

What Is the Execution Log?

The **Execution Log** records every run of your workflows—successful or failed. It allows you to see:

- **Trigger Details** (when and why the workflow was triggered)
- **Node Execution Order**
- **Data Passed Between Nodes**
- **Error Messages and Debug Info**

Flowchart: Execution Log Workflow

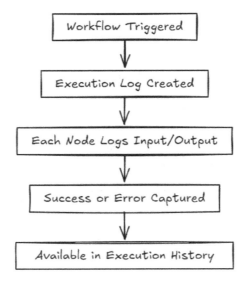

How to Access the Execution Log

To access logs in the n8n UI:

1. Open your workflow.
2. Click on the **"Executions"** tab at the top.
3. Select a specific execution from the list.
4. Click on any node in the visual timeline to inspect its data.

Understanding the Execution Log Interface

Feature	Description
Execution List	Shows a list of all workflow executions with timestamps and status.
Node Visualization	Nodes are color-coded (green = success, red = error).
Input Data	View the exact input received by a node during execution.
Output Data	See what data a node produced after it ran.
Error Messages	Displays errors if the node failed (e.g., "Missing credentials").
Rerun Button	Allows you to rerun the same execution.

Example Table: Execution Status Codes

Status	Meaning	Typical Use Case
Success	Workflow completed with no errors	Expected output achieved.
Error	One or more nodes failed	Invalid config or external API issue.
Waiting	Waiting for external input or time	Delayed webhook or scheduled start.
Canceled	Stopped manually or timed out	Execution interrupted or exceeded time.

Debugging Using the Execution Log

Step-by-Step Debug Process:

1. **Identify the Error Node**: Look for red nodes in the visual timeline.
2. **Click the Node**: Open its details to see the exact input, output, and error message.
3. **Check Input/Output**: Compare expected vs. actual data.
4. **Review Dependencies**: Check previous nodes for possible misconfiguration or incorrect data flow.
5. **Fix and Rerun**: Modify the workflow as needed, then rerun the failed execution directly.

Best Practices for Execution Logs

Practice	Benefit
Enable full logging	Helps capture rich input/output data.

Use version control for workflows	Easier to track changes across executions.
Regularly clean old executions	Improves performance and avoids clutter.
Use descriptive node names	Makes reading logs and debugging simpler.

Key Takeaways

- The Execution Log is your central tool for reviewing, debugging, and improving workflows.
- Use input/output inspection to trace data flow and errors.
- Leverage rerun and execution history to test fixes without starting from scratch.

Chapter 2: n8n Fundamentals

This chapter introduces the foundational building blocks of n8n—**nodes, triggers, actions**, and how **data flows** between them in **JSON format**. Understanding these concepts is crucial to building reliable, scalable, and dynamic automations.

Learning Objectives

By the end of this chapter, you will be able to:

- Differentiate between **nodes, triggers**, and **actions**.
- Understand the **anatomy of a node** and how nodes interact.
- Comprehend how **data flows** between nodes.
- Interpret and manipulate **JSON data**, the core data structure in n8n.

2.1 Nodes, Triggers, and Actions

What Is a Node in n8n?

A **node** is a building block of an n8n workflow. Each node performs a specific function—like making an API call, sending an email, filtering data, or executing code.

Types of Nodes

Node Type	Description	Examples
Trigger Node	Starts the workflow when an event occurs	Webhook, Cron, Gmail Trigger
Action Node	Performs an operation on received data	HTTP Request, Send Email, Slack

Logic Node	Implements conditions or flow control	IF, Switch, Merge
Function Node	Executes custom JavaScript	Custom data transformation
Set Node	Sets or modifies data fields	Create static or calculated data

Flowchart: Node Relationship

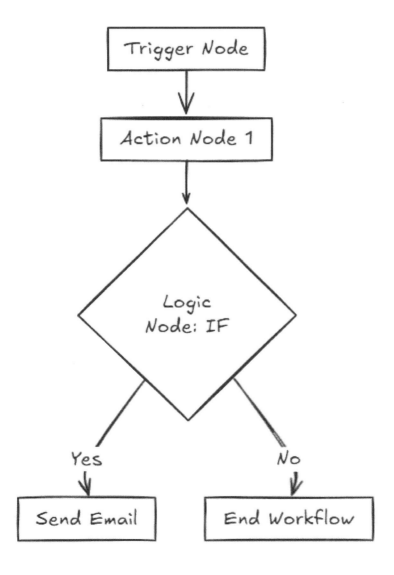

Triggers vs Actions

Aspect	Trigger	Action
Purpose	Starts a workflow	Executes a task
Example	New email in Gmail	Send message to Slack
Frequency	Event-based or scheduled	Executes every time it's triggered

Key Takeaways

- **Nodes** are the building blocks of workflows.
- A **Trigger** starts the automation; **Actions** and **Logic** nodes process data.
- Organizing nodes with logical flow leads to cleaner, more efficient automations.

2.2 Data Flow & JSON Fundamentals

Understanding Data Flow in n8n

Data flows **sequentially** from one node to the next. Each node receives **input data**, processes it, and outputs a **new JSON object**. Nodes can pass:

- A **single item**
- An **array of items**
- Complex, nested **JSON structures**

Flowchart: Data Movement Between Nodes

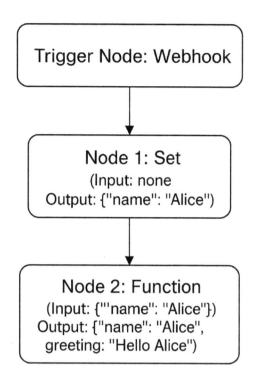

JSON in n8n

JSON (JavaScript Object Notation) is the data format used internally by n8n. Every node sends and receives data in JSON.

Sample JSON Object in n8n

```
{

"name": "Alice",

"email": "alice@example.com",

"subscribed": true

}
```

Common JSON Data Structures

Structure	Example	Description
Object	{ "key": "value" }	A set of key–value pairs
Array	[{ "name": "A" }, { "name": "B" }]	A list of objects
Nested Object	{ "user": { "name": "Alice" } }	Object inside an object
Boolean/Number	{ "active": true, "count": 5 }	Basic data types

Step-by-Step: Tracking JSON Flow

1. **Trigger** receives initial input (e.g., form submission).
2. **Set Node** defines fields or constants.
3. **Function Node** manipulates the data with JavaScript.
4. **HTTP Request Node** sends modified JSON to an API.
5. **Response** is processed and passed to the next node.

Best Practices for Managing Data

Tip	Benefit
Use the **Set Node** early	Structure and clean data before usage
Use **Descriptive Keys**	Makes workflows readable and manageable

Use **Function Node** sparingly	Keeps logic simple and maintainable
Monitor with **Execution Logs**	View how data changes step by step

Key Takeaways

- n8n uses **JSON** to structure and transfer data.
- Data flows linearly from node to node unless controlled by logic.
- Knowing how to manipulate JSON is essential to building functional workflows.

2.3 Using Expressions and Variables

n8n expressions allow you to dynamically reference and manipulate data using variables and functions. This section explores how expressions work and how to use them to make workflows more powerful and flexible.

Key Learning Objectives

- Understand the syntax of n8n expressions.
- Learn how to access node data using variables.
- Apply built-in functions for data transformation.
- Master dynamic field population using expressions.

Expression Syntax Overview

Expressions in n8n are written in {{ ... }} and use JavaScript-like syntax.

Example: {{ $json["email"] }}

This expression fetches the email field from the JSON output of the current node.

Commonly Used Variables

Variable	Description

$json	Accesses the JSON data of the current item
$node["NodeName"].json	Accesses output of another node
$items()	Retrieves all items from previous nodes
$now	Current date/time
$env	Access environment variables

Table: Example Expressions

Use Case	Expression	Description
Get user's name	{{ $json["name"] }}	Extracts the name field
Format a date	{{ new Date().toISOString() }}	Returns current date in ISO format
Access value from another node	{{ $node["Webhook"].json["email"] }}	Gets email from Webhook node
Create full name	{{ $json["firstName"] + " " + $json["lastName"] }}	Concatenates two fields

Best Practices

Tip	Why It Matters
Use **descriptive node names**	Makes expressions easier to read and maintain
Validate expressions with preview	Avoid runtime errors due to undefined values
Use **Set** before expressions	Prepare data explicitly to avoid path confusion

Key Takeaways

- Expressions give workflows dynamic behavior.
- You can reference any node's output using $node["Name"].
- Combine expressions with logic to create adaptive workflows.

2.4 Input/Output Mapping & Data Chaining

In n8n, **data chaining** allows one node's output to become the input for another. Proper **input/output mapping** ensures the right data is passed through the workflow for correct execution.

Learning Objectives

- Understand how data is passed between nodes.
- Map specific fields from one node to another.
- Chain nodes to build dynamic, logical workflows.

What is Data Chaining?

Data chaining is the process of **linking multiple nodes** where the **output of one becomes the input of another**.

Flowchart: Data Chaining

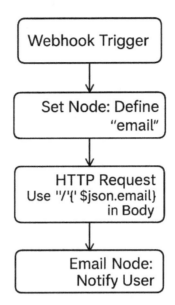

Understanding Input/Output Mapping

Each node can receive data from:

- **Previous Node**
- **Multiple Nodes** (if merged)
- **Static Input** (manually defined fields)

You can map data using:

- **Direct Mapping**: Select fields in the UI
- **Expression-Based Mapping**: Use {{ $json["fieldName"] }}

Table: Mapping Strategies

Scenario	Method	Example
Direct copy of a field	Expression	{{ $json["email"] }}

Combine two fields	Expression	{{ $json["first"] + " " + $json["last"] }}
Add constant value	Set Node	{{ "Active" }}
Use value from previous node	$node["NodeName"].json["field"]	{{ $node["Set"].json["email"] }}

Troubleshooting Data Chains

Problem	Likely Cause	Solution
Undefined value in expression	Incorrect path or node reference	Double-check field names and node output
Empty output	Previous node failed or was skipped	Review execution log
Incorrect mapping	Data mismatch or wrong structure	Use **Set** node to reshape data

Key Takeaways

- Each node passes structured data (usually JSON) to the next.
- Use expressions to map specific data fields.
- Proper chaining is essential for workflow accuracy and efficiency.

2.5 Environment Variables and Static Data

In n8n, environment variables and static data allow you to configure reusable values and settings across workflows, making them more scalable, secure, and environment-agnostic. This section explains how to define, access, and apply these data types efficiently.

Learning Objectives

- Understand what environment variables and static data are.
- Learn how to use environment variables for secrets and configuration.
- Use static data to store persistent workflow-level data.
- Apply these features in real-world use cases.

Environment Variables in n8n

Environment variables are values set outside the workflow but accessed inside it using expressions. They are useful for secrets, tokens, or custom configuration.

Use Cases

- API keys or tokens
- URLs for third-party services
- Enabling or disabling features

Flowchart: How Environment Variables Work

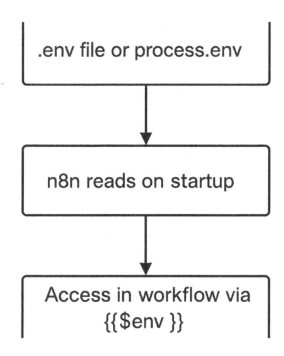

Table: Common Environment Variable Examples

Variable Name	Description	Example Value
N8N_BASIC_AUTH_USER	Username for basic auth	admin
N8N_BASIC_AUTH_PASS WORD	Password for basic auth	secure123
N8N_HOST	Host URL for the instance	localhost
N8N_PORT	Port on which n8n runs	5678
N8N_PERSONALIZED_API	Custom key or config used in workflow	my-api-key-12345

Accessing Environment Variables in Workflows

You can use the $env variable to access these values:

Example:

```
{{ $env["N8N_PERSONALIZED_API"] }}
```

Best Practice: Store tokens and secrets as environment variables rather than hardcoding them.

Static Data in Workflows

Static data is stored within the workflow and persists between executions. It's useful for saving state, counters, or configuration that shouldn't change frequently.

When to Use Static Data

- Store a last run timestamp.
- Maintain execution counters.

- Save values across multiple workflow runs.

Setting Static Data

You can modify static data via the Function or FunctionItem node:

```
// Example: Store counter

const count = $workflow.staticData;

count.counter = (count.counter || 0) + 1;

return items;
```

Reading Static Data

```
// Access counter

const count = $workflow.staticData.counter;
```

Flowchart: Static Data Lifecycle

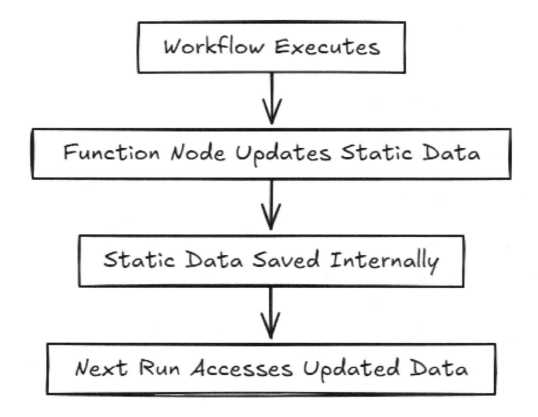

Table: Comparison – Env Vars vs. Static Data

Feature	Environment Variables	Static Data
Scope	Global to n8n instance	Local to workflow
Use Case	Config, secrets	Persistent internal values
Access Method	{{ $env["KEY"] }}	$workflow.staticData
Persistence	External, loaded on startup	Internal, stored with workflow
Security	Secure if .env is protected	Limited to workflow context

Key Takeaways

- **Environment Variables** keep configuration and secrets out of workflows.
- **Static Data** helps maintain persistent values like counters or last processed IDs.
- Using both strategically improves reusability, security, and scalability.

Chapter 3: Working with Triggers

Chapter Objective

Understand how triggers initiate workflows in n8n, and learn to configure and apply webhook and time-based triggers for real-world automation.

3.1 Webhooks

Webhooks allow n8n to receive real-time data from external services and trigger workflows based on events like form submissions, app notifications, or API calls.

Learning Objectives

- Learn what a webhook is and how it works.
- Understand how to create a webhook trigger in n8n.
- Explore real-world examples and best practices.

Flowchart: Webhook Workflow Lifecycle

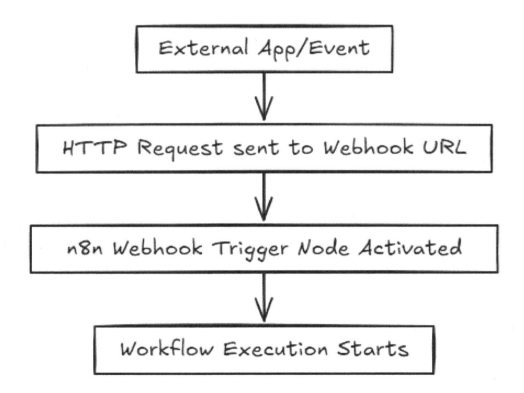

Step-by-Step: Setting Up a Webhook Trigger

1. **Create a new workflow in n8n.**
2. **Add a "Webhook" node** as the trigger.
3. **Choose the HTTP method** (GET, POST, etc.).
4. **Copy the generated Webhook URL.**
5. **Send a test request** to the URL from an external app or tool (e.g., Postman).
6. **Click "Execute Workflow" in n8n.**
7. **n8n captures the request data** and triggers the workflow.

Table: Webhook Configuration Options

Option	Description	Example
HTTP Method	Request type to listen for	POST, GET, PUT
Path	Unique endpoint identifier	/form-submit
Response Mode	When and how to respond to sender	On Received, Last Node
Response Code	HTTP status to return	200, 201
Response Body	Data returned to the external app	{ "status": "received" }

Best Practices

- Use **unique paths** for each webhook to avoid conflicts.
- Validate incoming data before processing.
- Secure with authentication (e.g., token or IP filtering).
- Use **Response Mode: Last Node** for async operations.

3.2 Cron and Scheduled Jobs

Scheduled triggers automate tasks on a recurring basis using time intervals—daily, weekly, hourly, or even to the second.

Learning Objectives

- Understand what a Cron trigger is.
- Set up time-based automation using n8n.
- Implement recurring workflows like backups or reports.

Flowchart: Cron-Based Workflow

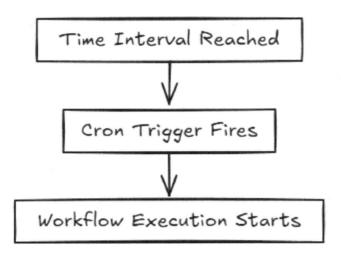

Step-by-Step: Creating a Scheduled Job

1. **Create a new workflow in n8n.**
2. **Add the "Cron" node** as the trigger.
3. **Select Mode**: Basic or Custom.
4. **In Basic Mode**:
   - Choose interval (e.g., daily at 9:00 AM).
5. **In Custom Mode**:
   - Enter a cron expression (e.g., 0 0 * * 1 for every Monday at midnight).
6. **Add additional nodes to define the job.**
7. **Activate the workflow.**

Table: Cron Trigger Modes

Mode	Use Case	Example
Basic	Common intervals	Daily at 08:00
Custom	Advanced, cron expression needed	0 0 * * * (every midnight)

Common Cron Expressions

Expression	Meaning
* * * * *	Every minute
0 * * * *	Hourly
0 0 * * *	Daily at midnight
0 9 * * 1-5	Weekdays at 9:00 AM
0 0 1 * *	First day of each month

Best Practices

- For critical tasks, **log execution status** to a file or external system.
- Use **Custom Mode** for flexibility with business schedules.
- Combine with **error handling nodes** for reliability.

Key Takeaways

- **Webhooks** enable real-time, event-driven workflows.
- **Cron triggers** automate repetitive tasks on defined schedules.
- Proper configuration ensures stability and performance.

3.3 Polling APIs and Events

Polling is a method where n8n periodically checks an external API or service for changes or new data. Unlike webhooks, it's not real-time but is useful when APIs don't support callbacks.

Learning Objectives

- Understand the concept and use case of polling.
- Learn how to configure polling using the **HTTP Request** and **IF** nodes.
- Apply polling for APIs that lack webhook support.

Flowchart: Polling API for New Events

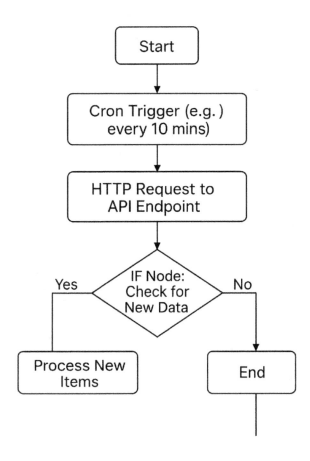

Step-by-Step: Implementing Polling

1. **Add a Cron node** to define the polling interval (e.g., every 10 minutes).
2. **Add an HTTP Request node** to call the external API.
3. **Use an IF node** to compare new data against previous results (e.g., last item timestamp).
4. **Process data** only if it's new.
5. **Store the last fetched timestamp or ID** using static data or an external data store (like Airtable or Redis).

Table: API Polling Setup Example

Component	Description	Example
API Endpoint	URL to request data from	https://api.example.com/orders
Cron Frequency	Interval between each API call	Every 15 minutes
Response Format	Expected JSON response	{ "orders": [...] }
Filtering Logic	Check if data is newer than the last call	Compare created_at timestamps
State Storage	Where to store last item fetched	n8n static data / external DB

Best Practices

- Avoid polling too frequently to reduce API rate limits and latency.
- Implement **error handling** for failed API requests.
- Store **polling state** (last item ID, timestamp) to prevent duplicate processing.
- Use **deduplication** logic inside workflows.

3.4 External App Triggers

Many SaaS platforms integrate natively with n8n using pre-built trigger nodes (e.g., Airtable Trigger, Google Sheets Trigger). These allow event-based automation without configuring raw webhooks.

Learning Objectives

- Identify external apps with native n8n trigger support.
- Learn how to configure triggers with authentication and event selection.
- Compare native triggers vs manual webhook setups.

Flowchart: External App Trigger

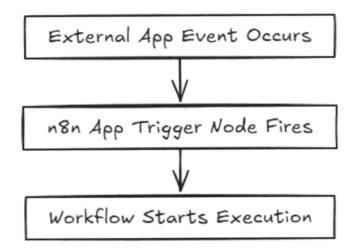

Step-by-Step: Using External App Triggers

1. **Create a new workflow.**
2. **Add a supported app's trigger node**, such as:
   - **Airtable Trigger**
   - **Google Sheets Trigger**
   - **Gmail Trigger**
3. **Connect your account** via OAuth or API key.
4. **Select trigger event** (e.g., New Row, New Email).
5. **Test the trigger** by simulating or performing an event in the app.
6. **Continue building your workflow based on the received data.**

Table: Common External App Triggers in n8n

App	Trigger Event Examples	Use Case Example
Airtable	New Record, Updated Record	When a new task is added to a table
Google Sheets	New Row, Row Updated	Auto-send email when row is added
Gmail	New Email Received	Notify Slack when new email is received
Slack	New Message, Channel Event	Log new messages to Notion
Trello	New Card, Card Moved	Track project board changes

Best Practices

- Use **OAuth** for secure connections.
- Limit triggers to specific conditions (e.g., certain folders or tables).
- Use **Filter and Switch** nodes to handle specific event types.
- Monitor API quotas for connected apps.

Key Takeaways

- **Polling** is ideal for APIs without webhooks but requires deduplication logic.
- **External App Triggers** provide simple, native integrations without custom endpoints.
- Use polling and external app triggers **strategically** depending on app capability and workflow need.

3.5 Real-Time vs Delayed Automation

In workflow automation, understanding the **timing** of execution is crucial. Automations can be **real-time** (instant) or **delayed** (scheduled, polled, or manually triggered). n8n supports both models, and choosing the right one affects performance, user experience, and system reliability.

Learning Objectives

- Distinguish between **real-time** and **delayed** workflows.
- Understand when to use **each automation type**.
- Learn how n8n implements both methods using **trigger nodes** and **schedulers**.
- Evaluate performance and reliability trade-offs.

Flowchart: Choosing Automation Timing

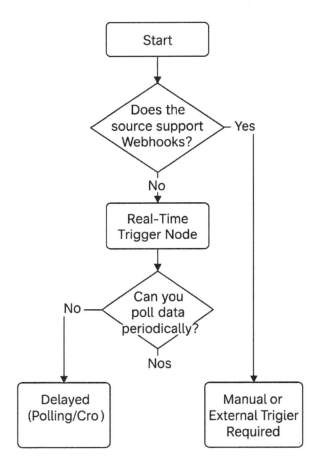

Real-Time Automation

Real-time automation responds **instantly** to events using **webhooks** or **native app triggers**.

Common Use Cases:

- New form submission via Typeform.
- Payment completed via Stripe.
- New email received in Gmail.

Pros:

- Instant response.
- Lower resource usage (event-driven).
- Ideal for user-facing actions.

Cons:

- Requires apps to support webhooks.
- Network reliability becomes critical.
- More complex to test during development.

Delayed Automation

Delayed automation uses **time-based schedules** (Cron) or **polling** methods to check for changes.

Common Use Cases:

- Daily report generation.
- Checking for new database entries every hour.
- Periodic sync between two platforms.

Pros:

- Works with APIs that lack webhook support.
- Easier to test and control frequency.
- Useful for batching tasks.

Cons:

- Not instant.
- May increase API usage and latency.
- Requires deduplication logic.

Comparison Table: Real-Time vs Delayed Automation

Feature	Real-Time	Delayed (Polling / Scheduled)
Trigger Mechanism	Webhook / App Trigger	Cron Node / Polling API
Response Time	Immediate	Minutes to hours
Reliability	Depends on external events	Controlled by internal scheduling
Setup Complexity	Medium (requires webhook setup)	Low to Medium
Use Case Example	Send email on new Typeform entry	Generate weekly report
API Usage Impact	Low (event-driven)	Higher (frequent API calls)

Step-by-Step: Switching Between Modes

To Convert Delayed to Real-Time:

1. Replace **Cron + HTTP Request** with a **Webhook Trigger**.
2. Point the source application to the webhook URL.
3. Adjust downstream logic to handle immediate responses.

To Convert Real-Time to Delayed:

1. Use a **Cron Node** to schedule periodic triggers.
2. Replace webhook trigger with an **HTTP Request** to poll the API.
3. Add **IF Node** to filter already-processed items.

Best Practices

- Always prefer **real-time** automation when the app supports webhooks.
- Use **delayed** automation for reporting, data syncs, and non-urgent tasks.
- Implement **retry and error handling** logic for both types to ensure reliability.
- Use **environment variables** to control timing without modifying the workflow.

Key Takeaways

- **Real-time automation** is fast and efficient but depends on webhook support.
- **Delayed automation** provides flexibility and broad compatibility but requires thoughtful design.
- Choose the right timing model based on the **application's capability**, **business needs**, and **resource constraints**.

Chapter 4: Core Nodes and Logic

Chapter Objectives

- Understand the core nodes available in n8n and how to use them for various tasks.
- Learn how to incorporate logic (conditional, data manipulation, etc.) into workflows.
- Master the use of advanced logic nodes like Function, FunctionItem, and IF conditions.

4.1 HTTP Request and API Calls

The **HTTP Request node** is one of the most powerful tools in n8n. It allows you to connect to **any RESTful API**, enabling integration with services that don't yet have native support in n8n.

Learning Objectives

- Understand how to configure the **HTTP Request node**.
- Learn the structure of **GET, POST, PUT, DELETE** requests.
- Send authenticated requests (API Key, OAuth2, Bearer Token).
- Handle API responses and errors effectively.

Table: Common HTTP Methods

Method	Purpose	Use Case Example
GET	Retrieve data	Fetch a list of users from CRM
POST	Create data	Add a new contact to mailing list
PUT	Update existing data	Update task in project manager

DELETE	Remove data	Delete a record from a database

Step-by-Step: Making an API Call

Example: GET Request to JSONPlaceholder API

1. **Add HTTP Request Node**
2. Set **Method** to GET
3. Set **URL** to https://jsonplaceholder.typicode.com/posts
4. Leave other fields as default
5. Run the node to see response data

Flowchart: HTTP Request Workflow

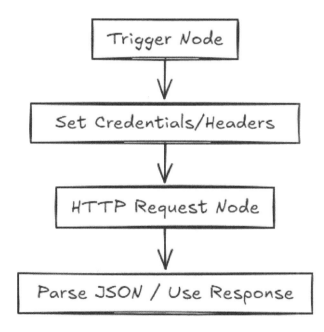

Authentication Methods Supported

Auth Type	Description	Setup Example
No Auth	Open APIs or local services	Public REST APIs

API Key	API key in header or query param	?apikey=12345
OAuth2	Secure authentication with tokens	Google, Microsoft, Slack
Bearer Token	Token in Authorization header	Authorization: Bearer TOKEN123
Basic Auth	Username + Password	REST APIs requiring login

Tips

- Use **Set Node** to define dynamic headers or query parameters.
- Catch and inspect errors using the **Error Trigger Node**.
- Combine with the **IF Node** for response validation.

Key Takeaways

- The HTTP Request Node is your gateway to external systems.
- Use the right HTTP method and authentication.
- Handle responses and errors gracefully.

4.2 Function and FunctionItem Nodes (JavaScript)

The **Function** and **FunctionItem** nodes allow custom scripting in **JavaScript**, providing ultimate flexibility within workflows.

Learning Objectives

- Understand when to use **Function** vs **FunctionItem**.
- Write custom JS to transform, enrich, or validate data.
- Access item properties, global variables, and environment values.

Difference Between Function and FunctionItem

Node Type	Processes	Ideal Use Case
Function	All items at once	Data aggregation, conditional branching
FunctionItem	One item at a time	Modify or enrich individual items

Basic FunctionItem Example

```
// This will run for each item individually

item.myField = item.myField.toUpperCase();

return item;
```

Basic Function Example

```
// This runs once with access to all items

return items.map(item => {

  item.json.status = 'processed';

  return item;

});
```

Common Use Cases

Use Case	Node Type	Example
Convert text to lowercase	FunctionItem	item.name.toLowerCase()

Filter items based on condition	Function	if (item.value > 10)
Merge data from multiple sources	Function	combine JSON arrays from APIs

Flowchart: Function Node Workflow

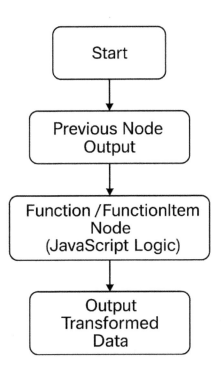

Tips for Writing JavaScript in n8n

- Use item.json.fieldName to access fields.
- Always return item or return items.
- Use console.log() for debugging (visible in Execution Logs).
- Remember: FunctionItem returns a **single object**; Function returns an **array**.

Key Takeaways

- Function nodes unlock **custom behavior** in workflows.
- Use **FunctionItem** for per-item changes; use **Function** for batch logic.
- Write clean, safe JavaScript, and test often.

4.3 Set, Merge, SplitInBatches Nodes

This section covers three core utility nodes: **Set**, **Merge**, and **SplitInBatches**. These nodes help you manipulate data, combine workflows, and process large datasets in manageable chunks.

Learning Objectives

- Learn to use the **Set node** to define or clean data.
- Understand **Merge node** strategies to combine data.
- Use **SplitInBatches** to paginate and loop through datasets.

Set Node: Defining and Cleaning Data

The **Set node** is used to:

- Add static fields.
- Rename or remove existing fields.
- Simplify output for downstream nodes.

Example Use Case:
Add a status label "processed" to every item.

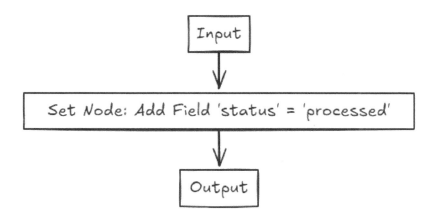

Set Node Table Example

Option	Description
Keep Only Set	Remove all other fields except the ones set
Add New Fields	Add custom key-value pairs to the item
Change Existing	Modify values of existing fields

Merge Node: Combining Data Streams

Use the **Merge node** to join two data streams. Merge strategies include:

Merge Mode	Description
Append	Concatenate two arrays of items
Merge by Index	Join items at the same index
Merge by Key	Match and merge items by a specific field name
Pass-Through	Combine one stream with unchanged data

Flowchart Example: Merging Two APIs

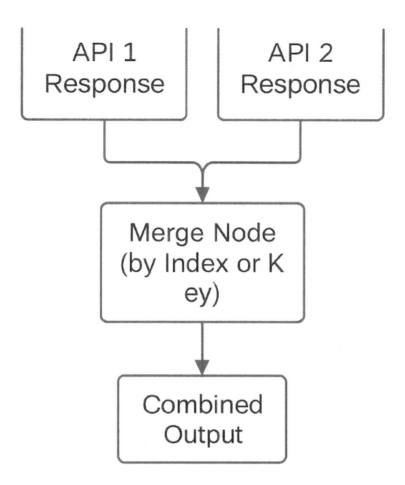

SplitInBatches Node: Looping Through Items

When working with large datasets or APIs with rate limits, use **SplitInBatches**.

Example Use Case:
Split 1000 items into groups of 50 and send emails one batch at a time.

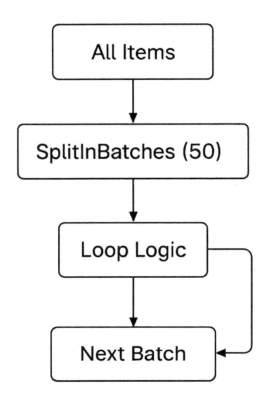

Tips:

- Combine with **Wait node** to pause between batches.
- Use **While loop** pattern with a **Continue On Fail** option for resilience.

Key Takeaways

- **Set node** is ideal for cleaning or defining data fields.
- **Merge node** helps consolidate multi-source data.
- **SplitInBatches** enables controlled loops over large datasets.

4.4 Conditional Logic: IF, Switch, Wait Nodes

n8n's logic-based nodes enable decision-making within workflows. These include **IF**, **Switch**, and **Wait**—essential for building dynamic, event-based automations.

Learning Objectives

- Use **IF** and **Switch** nodes for conditional branching.
- Employ the **Wait node** to pause workflows based on time or input.
- Understand how to combine conditions for complex scenarios.

IF Node: Binary Conditions

The **IF node** evaluates a condition and branches based on **true/false** outcomes.

Example:
If order.value > 100, send a VIP confirmation email.

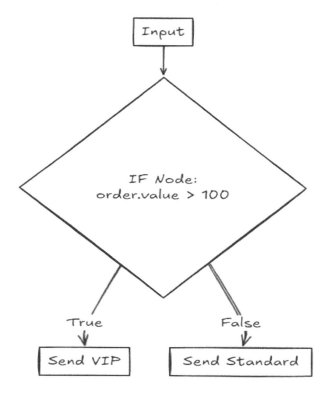

Supported Conditions

Condition Type	Example
String Comparison	email == 'test@example.com'

Number Comparison	price > 50
Boolean	isActive == true
Null/Undefined	status != null

Switch Node: Multi-Branch Conditions

The **Switch node** routes data based on **multiple values** of a field.

Use Case Example:
Route a support ticket based on priority.

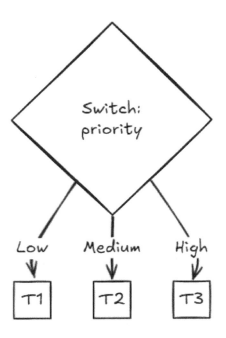

Wait Node: Pausing Execution

Use the **Wait node** to:

- Delay execution for a specific time (e.g., 5 minutes).
- Wait until a date/time (e.g., future reminder).
- Await a webhook or event (e.g., approval system).

Example Use Case: Delay a follow-up email by 2 days.

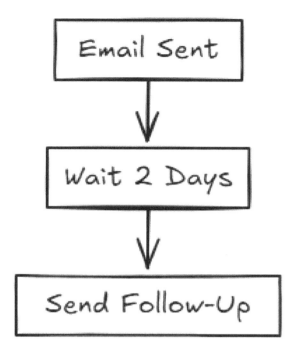

Key Takeaways

- **IF** handles binary logic (true/false).
- **Switch** handles multi-branch logic.
- **Wait** pauses workflow for time-based or event-based triggers.

4.5 Error Handling and Try-Catch Patterns

In any automation environment, errors are inevitable. n8n offers powerful built-in tools to detect, manage, and respond to errors using **error workflows**, **conditional logic**, and **try-catch patterns**. This section will teach you how to make your workflows more resilient and reliable.

Learning Objectives

- Understand how n8n handles errors at the node and workflow level.
- Implement try-catch logic using nodes and conditional flows.
- Design fallback mechanisms and alert systems for failed automations.

Understanding Error Propagation in n8n

When a node fails:

- Execution **stops** unless "Continue on Fail" is enabled.
- The **error message and stack trace** are logged in the execution log.
- You can **route the error** to a separate branch using **Error Triggers** or **conditional nodes**.

Error Handling Techniques Table

Technique	Description
Continue on Fail	Allows workflow to continue even if a node fails.
Error Trigger Workflow	Starts a separate workflow when any other workflow fails.
Conditional Error Path	Use IF or Switch nodes to route execution after potential failure.
Notifications	Send alerts via email, Slack, or webhook on failure.
Retry Logic	Reattempt the failed step using Loops or Wait node with condition.

Try-Catch Pattern in n8n

While n8n does not have a built-in "try/catch" function, you can replicate the logic using standard nodes.

Flowchart: Try-Catch-Finally

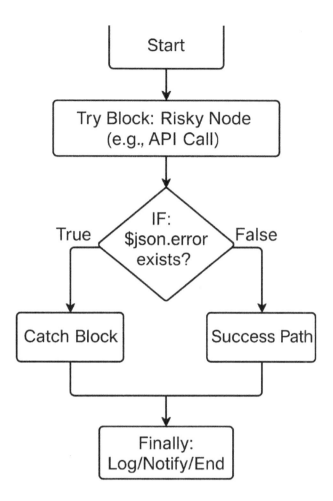

Step-by-Step Try-Catch Implementation

1. **Try Block:**
   ○ Add the node that may fail.
   ○ Enable **"Continue on Fail"**.
2. **Catch Block:**
   ○ Add an **IF node** to check if the node output has an error (e.g., check for empty data or status code).
3. **Alternative Action:**
   ○ Send a notification, retry the action, or trigger a fallback workflow.
4. **Finally Block:**
   ○ Use **Set node** to flag the error or log the result.
   ○ Optional: Add an HTTP Request node to send logs to an external service.

Retry and Timeout Strategy with Wait

Add a **Loop** and **Wait node** between retries.

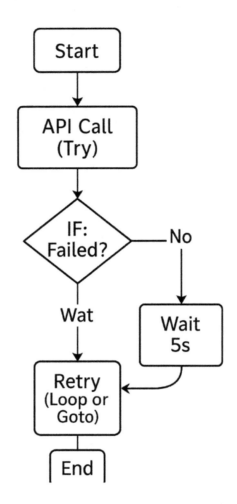

Error Trigger Workflow

The **Error Trigger node** can run a separate workflow when any other workflow fails.

Use Case: Centralized error logging and alerting.

Node	Role
Error Trigger	Entry point for all workflow failures

Set	Capture failed workflow name and error message
Slack/Email	Notify team
HTTP	Log error to monitoring system

Key Takeaways

- Use **"Continue on Fail"** to prevent full workflow halts.
- Simulate **try/catch logic** using IF nodes and conditional paths.
- Combine **Wait**, **Loop**, and **Switch** nodes for custom retry logic.
- Use **Error Trigger** workflows to centralize alerting and recovery.

Chapter 5: Workflow Design Patterns

Chapter Objectives

- Understand modular design principles for creating scalable and maintainable workflows.
- Learn how to use sub-workflows to simplify complex automation tasks.
- Master the management of workflow complexity and ensure performance optimization.
- Explore reusability with templates and how to streamline your automation process.

5.1 Modular Workflow Design

As workflows grow in complexity, organizing them into **modular, reusable components** becomes essential. Modular design improves readability, scalability, and maintenance. In this section, you'll learn how to design workflows that are both efficient and easy to manage.

Learning Objectives

- Understand the principles of modular workflow design.
- Learn best practices for organizing and structuring workflows.
- Identify when to split large workflows into smaller components.

Principles of Modular Design

Principle	Description
Reusability	Break common patterns into repeatable blocks or sub-workflows.
Separation of Concerns	Keep logic for different functions or processes in separate nodes/flows.
Scalability	Structure workflows so that they can grow without becoming unwieldy.

Maintainability	Make workflows easy to understand, debug, and update.

Modular Workflow Flowchart

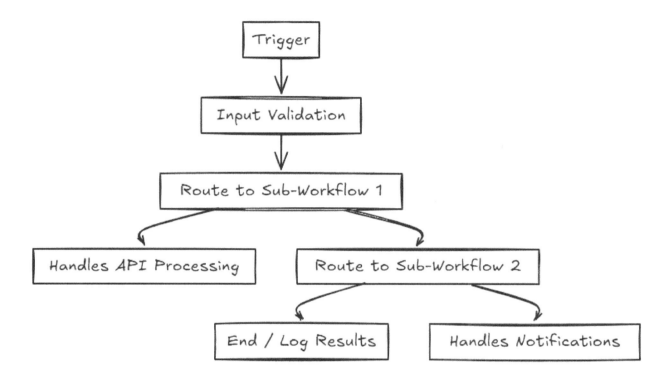

Step-by-Step Guide to Modular Design

1. **Identify Common Tasks**
   Look for repeated sequences (e.g., data formatting, notifications).
2. **Group Related Logic**
   Use distinct areas of the workflow or separate workflows to handle each concern.
3. **Use Naming Conventions**
   Name nodes and workflows clearly to indicate their purpose (e.g., Validate Input, Send Alert).
4. **Avoid Over-Nesting Logic**
   Minimize complexity within a single workflow. Delegate to sub-workflows where needed.
5. **Use Comments and Notes**
   Use the **Note** node in n8n to document important parts of the logic.

Design Best Practices Table

Best Practice	Why It Matters
Use sub-workflows for large logic	Keeps primary workflows clean and focused.
Keep triggers simple	Triggers should only validate and dispatch, not handle all logic.
Build for reusability	General-purpose logic should be abstracted and reused.
Comment critical paths	Helps future editors understand logic.
Test in isolation	Test modules individually before integrating them.

Example Use Case: Customer Onboarding Workflow

- **Trigger:** New form submission
- **Step 1:** Validate customer data
- **Step 2:** Check CRM for duplicates
- **Step 3:** Send welcome email
- **Step 4:** Add task to sales pipeline

Split the steps into **modules or sub-workflows** to reuse validation or CRM-check logic in other workflows.

Key Takeaways

- Modular workflows are easier to build, test, and maintain.
- Split large workflows into meaningful, functional blocks.
- Use clear naming, documentation, and structure to promote reusability.

5.2 Using Sub-Workflows and Workflow Triggers

Sub-workflows allow you to break down complex workflows into smaller, reusable pieces. This is especially useful when you have components of logic or actions that are used in multiple places. Workflow triggers help initiate sub-workflows from main workflows or between workflows. In this section, we'll explore how to structure and use sub-workflows effectively.

Learning Objectives

- Understand how to design workflows with sub-workflows.
- Learn how to trigger sub-workflows from a parent workflow.
- Discover how workflow triggers can be used for modular, reusable automation.

What Are Sub-Workflows?

A **sub-workflow** is essentially a workflow nested inside another workflow. It allows you to modularize your process into manageable parts, each responsible for a specific task or group of tasks.

How Sub-Workflows Work

1. **Main Workflow**: Initiates the overall process.
2. **Sub-Workflow**: Performs specific tasks (e.g., sending emails, updating databases).
3. **Workflow Trigger**: A special node that calls another workflow.

Sub-workflows are helpful for handling repetitive tasks, making them reusable, and improving maintainability. They can be triggered from anywhere, enabling dynamic workflow structures.

Using Sub-Workflows

Step	Action
1. Create Sub-Workflow	Break down a part of your process into a new workflow.
2. Add Workflow Trigger	In the parent workflow, use the "Execute Workflow" node to call the sub-workflow.

3. Pass Data	Use the "Set" node to pass inputs to the sub-workflow.
4. Execute & Return	Once the sub-workflow completes, return the results to the parent workflow for further processing.

Flowchart: Main Workflow Calling Sub-Workflow

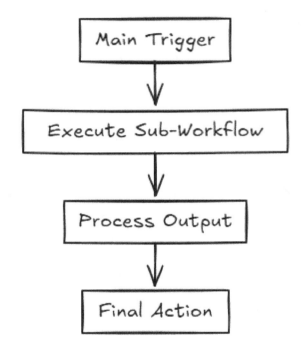

Example: Customer Registration Workflow with Sub-Workflows

In a **customer registration process**, the main workflow could be responsible for collecting the user's data. A sub-workflow can handle sending a confirmation email, while another handles logging the registration into a CRM system.

- **Main Workflow**: Collect form data and validate it.
- **Sub-Workflow 1**: Send confirmation email.
- **Sub-Workflow 2**: Add customer to CRM.

Both sub-workflows are triggered from the main workflow.

Workflow Trigger Node

- The **Execute Workflow** node is used to call a sub-workflow. It allows data from the parent workflow to be passed to the sub-workflow.
- Use the **Set** node before calling the sub-workflow to pass necessary data like user information or status.

Key Takeaways

- Sub-workflows improve workflow reusability and modularity.
- Use the **Execute Workflow** node to trigger sub-workflows.
- Passing data between workflows with **Set** nodes ensures seamless integration.

5.3 Managing Workflow Complexity

As workflows grow in size and complexity, they can become difficult to maintain, debug, and scale. This section covers strategies for managing and reducing workflow complexity, helping you build efficient, maintainable automations.

Learning Objectives

- Identify potential sources of complexity in workflows.
- Learn strategies for simplifying and optimizing workflows.
- Understand best practices for managing large workflows.

Sources of Workflow Complexity

Complexity in workflows often arises from:

1. **Overcrowded Workflows**: Too many nodes in a single workflow.
2. **Redundant Logic**: Repeating the same logic in multiple places.
3. **Nested Logic**: Deeply nested nodes that are hard to debug and maintain.
4. **Inefficient Data Handling**: Handling large datasets or frequent API calls inefficiently.

Simplifying Workflow Design

Tip	Description
Avoid Over-Crowded Workflows	Break down workflows into smaller, manageable sub-workflows.
Re-use Sub-Workflows	Modularize common tasks like data validation or notifications.
Limit Nested Logic	Use simple, clear logical flows (avoid deep nesting).
Optimize API Calls	Batch API calls or use caching when possible.
Use Data Transformation Nodes	Use **Set**, **Merge**, and **Function** nodes for efficient data manipulation.

Best Practices for Managing Workflow Complexity

1. **Subdivide Workflows**: Create sub-workflows for common tasks (e.g., database updates, notifications).
2. **Limit Conditional Nodes**: Keep conditional checks (IF/Switch) shallow to avoid unnecessary complexity.
3. **Use Functions for Reusability**: Store reusable code in **Function** or **FunctionItem** nodes.
4. **Optimize Node Execution**: Use **Batch**, **Wait**, or **Loop** nodes to manage repeated tasks.

Flowchart: Simplified Workflow Structure

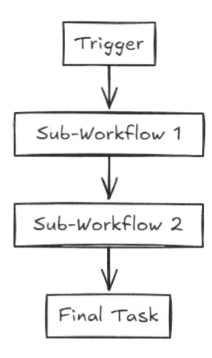

Example: Optimizing a Multi-Step Approval Process

Rather than having all approval logic within a single workflow, break the workflow into:

1. **Main Workflow**: Handles the approval trigger and sends initial request.
2. **Sub-Workflow 1**: Processes step 1 of approval (e.g., manager approval).
3. **Sub-Workflow 2**: Processes step 2 (e.g., finance team approval).
4. **Final Workflow**: Sends final approval or rejection notification.

This modular structure makes the workflow easier to manage, debug, and scale.

Key Takeaways

- Break down large workflows into sub-workflows to reduce complexity.
- Avoid deep nesting and redundant logic to improve readability and maintainability.
- Optimize API and data handling for efficiency.

5.4 Reusability and Templates

Reusability is a key principle in workflow automation. By building workflows that can be reused across different processes, you save time, reduce errors, and ensure consistency. n8n provides excellent tools for creating reusable workflows and templates that can be easily shared, modified, and applied in different scenarios.

Learning Objectives

- Understand the importance of reusability in workflow automation.
- Learn how to create reusable workflows and templates in n8n.
- Explore best practices for ensuring workflows remain adaptable for future use.

What Is Workflow Reusability?

Reusability means creating workflows or parts of workflows that can be used across different processes or projects. This reduces the need to build new workflows from scratch every time and helps you maintain consistency and efficiency.

Creating Reusable Workflows

1. **Modularize Logic**:
   Break your workflows into reusable components (sub-workflows) for tasks like sending emails, updating databases, or processing data.
2. **Use Workflow Templates**:
   n8n allows you to create **templates** that can be exported and reused in different projects. Templates are pre-built workflows that serve as a foundation for similar automation processes.

Steps to Create and Use Templates in n8n

Step	Action
1. Create a Workflow	Design a workflow that contains general-purpose logic.
2. Export Workflow	Export your workflow as a template for reuse or sharing.
3. Import Template	Import the template into a new project or workflow.

4. Modify as Needed	Customize the template according to the specific use case.

Workflow Template Example: Email Notification Template

- **Use Case**: Sending an email notification after a task is completed.
- **Template**: Create a template with a simple trigger (e.g., HTTP request), email body content, and recipients.
- **Customization**: Replace specific task data and recipient addresses as required for different projects.

Benefits of Using Reusable Templates

Benefit	Description
Consistency	Templates ensure that the same logic and structure are used.
Efficiency	Quickly deploy proven workflows without needing to start from scratch.
Scalability	Easily adapt workflows for new projects without major modifications.
Collaboration	Share templates with teams for standardization across workflows.

Key Takeaways

- Modular design and templates make workflows reusable, reducing effort and ensuring consistency.
- Workflow templates allow for quick deployment and collaboration across different projects.

- Use sub-workflows and set them up as templates for recurring tasks.

5.5 Performance Optimization Best Practices

Efficient workflows are crucial for performance, especially as workflows grow in size and complexity. Poorly optimized workflows can result in long execution times, high resource consumption, or failures. In this section, we'll look at strategies for improving the performance of your n8n workflows.

Learning Objectives

- Learn key performance bottlenecks in n8n workflows.
- Discover best practices for optimizing workflow performance.
- Understand how to monitor and troubleshoot performance issues.

Common Performance Issues in n8n

Issue	Description
High API Call Frequency	Excessive API calls or large payloads can slow down workflows.
Large Datasets	Working with large datasets can cause memory or processing bottlenecks.
Excessive Workflow Branching	Overcomplicating workflows with too many branches can lead to inefficiency.
Heavy Use of Loops	Unoptimized loops can lead to performance degradation.

Optimizing Workflow Performance

1. **Limit API Calls**:
   Use batching or aggregation techniques to reduce the number of API calls. Also, leverage API caching when possible.
2. **Reduce Data Handling Overhead**:
   Avoid passing large amounts of data between nodes unnecessarily. Filter and minimize data before passing it to other nodes.
3. **Avoid Deeply Nested Loops**:
   Instead of deeply nested loops, split large processes into smaller sub-workflows and execute them sequentially.
4. **Use Wait Nodes Strategically**:
   The **Wait** node can help stagger resource-intensive operations to prevent overloading the system or API rate limits.

Best Practices for Performance Optimization

Practice	Description
Batch Processing	Combine multiple tasks or API calls into batches.
Use Filters	Filter data early in the workflow to avoid unnecessary steps.
Use Wait Node Wisely	Add delays when necessary to avoid hitting limits or bottlenecks.
Minimize Workflow Branching	Limit the use of parallel branches to reduce complexity.
Optimize Node Execution	Use **Loop** and **Set** nodes efficiently, and avoid redundant operations.

Flowchart: Optimized Workflow

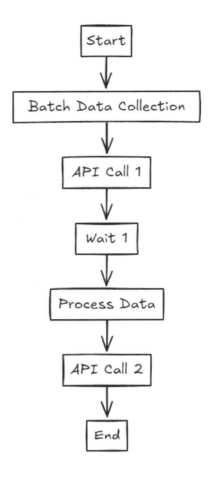

Example: Optimizing API Calls

Instead of making multiple individual API requests, **batch them into one request** (if the API supports batch operations), reducing the number of calls and minimizing overhead.

- **Non-Optimized Approach**:
  - API Call 1: Get customer data.
  - API Call 2: Get product data.
  - API Call 3: Get order data.
- **Optimized Approach**:
  - Single API Call: Get customer, product, and order data in one batch request.

Key Takeaways

- Performance optimization is crucial to ensure workflows run efficiently and scale.
- Focus on reducing API calls, optimizing data handling, and minimizing unnecessary workflow branches.

- Use batch processing, strategic waits, and simple structures to keep workflows fast and responsive.

Chapter 6: Integrations with Popular SaaS & Productivity Tools

Chapter Objectives

- Learn how to integrate n8n with commonly used SaaS tools for automation.
- Automate communication tools (email, Slack, Teams).
- Handle project management and collaboration tools (Trello, Asana, Notion).
- Manage document storage services (Google Sheets, Airtable).

6.1 Email Automation (Gmail, SMTP, Mailgun)

Email is one of the most widely used communication tools in automation. With n8n, automating email tasks like sending notifications, confirmations, and updates has never been easier. This section will guide you through integrating n8n with popular email platforms such as Gmail, SMTP, and Mailgun.

Learning Objectives

- Learn how to set up email automation with Gmail, SMTP, and Mailgun.
- Understand the process of sending, receiving, and managing email workflows in n8n.
- Explore advanced features such as dynamic email templates and error handling.

Integrating Gmail for Email Automation

1. **Setting Up Gmail Integration**:
   To connect Gmail with n8n, you need to authenticate via OAuth2. This process ensures secure access to your Gmail account for sending emails.

   Step-by-step Setup:
   - In n8n, add a **Gmail node** to your workflow.
   - Authenticate using Google OAuth2 credentials.
   - Configure the **Send Email** parameters:
     - **To**: Recipient email address.
     - **Subject**: Email subject.
     - **Text/HTML Content**: Email body content.

2. **Example Configuration:**

Field	Value
To	recipient@example.com
Subject	"Your Automation Result"
Body	"Here is the result..."

3. **Advanced Features**:
   - **Attachments**: Use dynamic data to attach files to the email.
   - **Templates**: Use expressions to dynamically build the email content based on incoming data (e.g., user names, dates).

SMTP Email Integration

SMTP is another powerful method for sending emails directly from n8n, using your preferred email server or a third-party service.

Step-by-step Setup:

- In n8n, add an **SMTP node** to your workflow.
- Configure the SMTP settings based on your email provider's specifications (e.g., SMTP server address, authentication details).

Common SMTP Settings:

Setting	Example Value
SMTP Server	smtp.mailtrap.io
SMTP Port	587

Authentication	Yes
Username	your_username
Password	your_password
From Address	youremail@example.com

Integrating Mailgun for Email Automation

Mailgun is a popular email automation service with advanced features for transactional emails, API-driven workflows, and high deliverability.

Step-by-step Setup:

- Add a **Mailgun node** to your workflow.
- Provide the API key and domain details for your Mailgun account.
- Configure the parameters for sending email

Field	Example Value
To	recipient@example.com
Subject	"Automated Email via Mailgun"
Body	"This is a transactional email."

API Key	key- XXXXXXXXXXXXXXXXXXXXXXXXXXX XXX
Domain	your-domain.mailgun.org

Key Takeaways

- Email automation with n8n can be achieved using Gmail, SMTP, and Mailgun integrations.
- Gmail uses OAuth2 for authentication, while SMTP relies on standard email server configurations.
- Mailgun offers advanced features such as templates, attachments, and easy API integrations.

6.2 Slack, Discord, MS Teams Bots

Bots are essential for modern workplace communication and collaboration. Slack, Discord, and Microsoft Teams are popular platforms for managing team interactions. n8n allows you to automate tasks by integrating with these platforms, sending messages, notifications, and alerts directly to your team.

Learning Objectives

- Set up Slack, Discord, and MS Teams bots to automate communication.
- Learn how to send messages, create channels, and manage team interactions through automation.
- Understand how to handle incoming messages and trigger workflows based on team interactions.

Slack Bot Integration

Slack bots can send notifications, create channels, and respond to messages based on workflow triggers.

Step-by-step Setup:

1. **Install Slack Node**:
    ○ In n8n, use the **Slack node** to connect with your Slack workspace.
    ○ Authenticate using the OAuth2 method with the Slack API.
2. **Send a Message**:
    ○ Configure the **Message** node to send messages to specific channels or direct messages.
    ○ Use **dynamic data** to personalize messages with workflow outputs.
3. **Example Configuration:**

Field	Value
Channel	#general
Message Text	"Hello, this is an automated message."
Attachments	"Image URL or file path"

Discord Bot Integration

Discord bots can automate communication in Discord servers, sending alerts, updates, or reminders.

Step-by-step Setup:

1. **Install Discord Node**:
    ○ Add the **Discord node** to your workflow.
    ○ Authenticate the bot using your Discord application token.
2. **Send a Message**:
    ○ Configure the **Send Message** action with channel details.
    ○ Use dynamic expressions to customize messages based on real-time data.

3. **Example Configuration:**

Field	Value
Channel ID	your_channel_id
Message	"New task completed!"

MS Teams Bot Integration

MS Teams offers integration for automating team communications and workflow alerts within your workspace.

Step-by-step Setup:

1. **Install MS Teams Node:**
   - Use the **MS Teams node** in n8n to authenticate with your organization's MS Teams account.
2. **Send a Message:**
   - Configure the node to send messages to teams, channels, or individuals, incorporating dynamic data for personalization.
3. **Example Configuration:**

Field	Value
Team	YourTeamName
Channel	General
Message	"Reminder: Update your tasks."

Advanced Features for All Platforms

- **Interactive Messages**: Send messages with buttons, links, or forms for interactive workflows.
- **Respond to User Inputs**: Capture responses from users and trigger subsequent actions based on their replies.
- **Broadcast Notifications**: Send bulk messages to multiple users or channels based on specific triggers.

Key Takeaways

- Slack, Discord, and MS Teams integration enables seamless communication automation within workflows.
- Automate messages, notifications, and interactive tasks with bots on each platform.
- Use dynamic data to personalize messages and respond to user inputs for more complex workflows.

6.3 Google Sheets, Excel, Airtable

Data storage and manipulation are essential in workflow automation. Tools like **Google Sheets**, **Microsoft Excel**, and **Airtable** act as dynamic databases for collecting, processing, and distributing information. n8n allows seamless integration with these tools for reading, writing, and automating data operations.

Learning Objectives

- Automate data entry and updates in Google Sheets, Excel, and Airtable.
- Trigger workflows based on spreadsheet changes or append data automatically.
- Learn the differences and use-cases for each tool in automation.

Comparison Table: Sheet-Based Tool Capabilities

Tool	Integration Method	Use Cases	Notes
Google Sheets	OAuth2	Form submissions, dynamic reports	Requires Google API setup

| Excel | Microsoft Graph API | Corporate reporting, internal ops | Needs MS 365 and Azure AD integration |
| Airtable | API Key / Token | Lightweight database workflows | Supports relational data structures |

Google Sheets Integration

Typical Use Case Flowchart

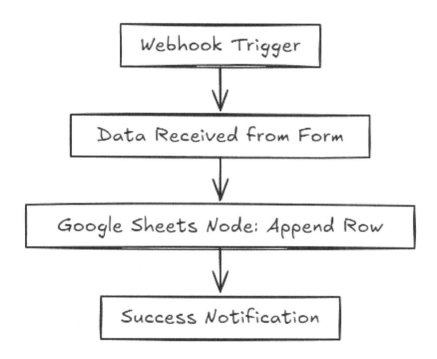

Steps to Integrate Google Sheets:

1. Add a **Google Sheets node**.
2. Authenticate with Google using OAuth2.
3. Choose an operation:
   - Append Row
   - Read Rows
   - Lookup Value
4. Use expressions to map incoming data fields to sheet columns.

Excel Integration (Microsoft 365)

Excel Online (via Microsoft Graph API) supports powerful business automation.

Steps to Connect Excel:

1. Add **Microsoft Excel node**.
2. Connect your Microsoft 365 account.
3. Choose spreadsheet and table.
4. Select operation (e.g., Add Row, Update Cell, Read Rows).

Example Table: Fields Mapped from n8n to Excel

Excel Column	Mapped Field from n8n
Name	{{$json["name"]}}
Email	{{$json["email"]}}
Status	{{$json["status"]}}

Airtable Integration

Airtable combines database flexibility with a spreadsheet interface.

Steps to Use Airtable Node:

1. Get your **API Key** from Airtable account.
2. Add **Airtable node** and authenticate.
3. Define the base and table to interact with.
4. Map fields dynamically using expressions.

Use Case: Workflow for Updating Airtable

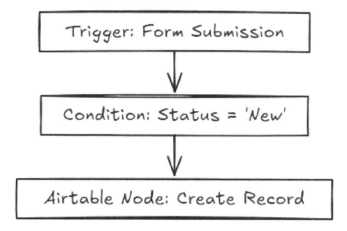

Key Takeaways

- Google Sheets and Excel are great for traditional spreadsheet workflows.
- Airtable supports more advanced structures like linked records and select fields.
- All three tools allow two-way data operations: read from and write to data stores.

6.4 Notion, Trello, Asana, ClickUp

Project and task management tools like **Notion**, **Trello**, **Asana**, and **ClickUp** are vital for organizing information and tracking workflows. n8n integrations allow you to create tasks, update statuses, and fetch project data programmatically.

Learning Objectives

- Learn how to automate task creation, status tracking, and documentation.
- Understand the unique features of each tool in relation to n8n.
- Automate daily standups, ticket updates, or documentation pipelines.

Comparison Table: Task Management Tools

Tool	Integration Type	Strengths	Limitations
Notion	OAuth2 / Token	Documentation + databases	Slower API, stricter data types

Trello	API Key + Token	Boards, cards, easy visuals	Flat data model
Asana	OAuth2	Task hierarchy, team projects	Rate-limited API
ClickUp	API Key	Highly customizable workflows	Complex config for beginners

Trello Integration

Example Flow: Task Creation

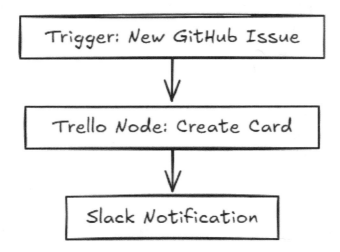

Steps to Set Up:

1. Add a **Trello node**.
2. Provide API Key and Token.
3. Choose board and list.
4. Map card title, description, due dates, and labels dynamically.

Asana Integration

Flowchart: Task Sync from CRM

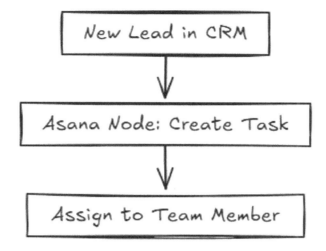

Steps:

1. Use **Asana node** with OAuth2 authentication.
2. Set task parameters (project, assignee, due date).
3. Automatically trigger updates or notifications as tasks progress.

Notion Integration

Flowchart: Log Notes from Email

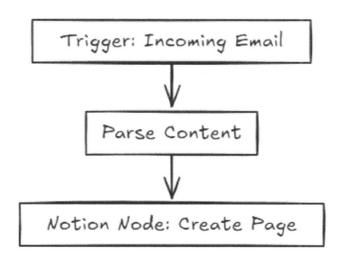

Steps to Use:

1. Use **Notion API token** or OAuth2.
2. Choose database or page as destination.
3. Map incoming data (email subject, sender, body) into structured blocks.

ClickUp Integration

Use Case: Automated Ticket Logging

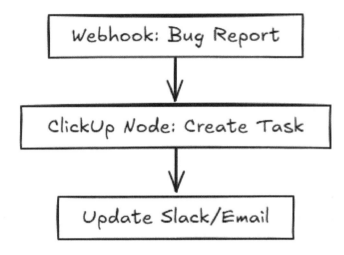

Steps:

1. Add **ClickUp node** and provide API Key.
2. Select workspace, space, folder, and list.
3. Populate task title, description, priority, assignee dynamically.

Key Takeaways

- Trello is ideal for visual task tracking; Asana excels in structured project management.
- Notion combines document management with databases.
- ClickUp provides full project lifecycle management and deep automation capability.

6.5 Calendar & Reminders

Integrating calendar tools into your workflows allows for effective scheduling, reminders, and time-based automation. Tools like **Google Calendar**, **Outlook Calendar**, and **iCal** can be used to automate meeting invites, reminders, and schedule-based triggers in n8n.

Learning Objectives

- Automate event creation and calendar-based workflows.
- Trigger actions based on scheduled events or upcoming dates.
- Manage reminders using calendar integrations.

Calendar Integration Flowchart

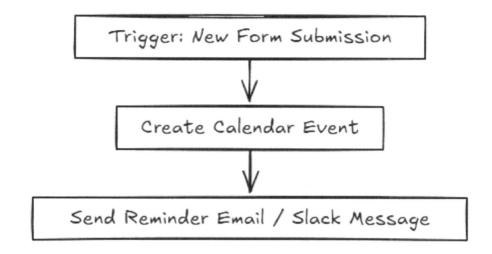

Supported Calendar Tools

Tool	Integration Type	Key Features	Limitations
Google Calendar	OAuth2	Easy to use, event-based triggers	Requires Google Cloud project
Microsoft Outlook	OAuth2	Enterprise-focused, Outlook events	May need Azure app registration
iCal	ICS Feed / URL	Lightweight, basic scheduling	Limited automation capabilities

Use Cases for Calendar Automation

- **Schedule reminders** based on form entries.
- **Sync calendar events** with external CRMs or productivity tools.
- **Trigger workflows** before/after events.

Example: Automating Event Reminders

1. Use **Cron or Calendar Trigger** to check upcoming events.
2. Filter events occurring in the next 24 hours.
3. Send an automated reminder (email, SMS, Slack).
4. Optionally, log activity in a spreadsheet or task manager.

Reminder Setup Table

Step	Node	Action
Trigger Event	Google Calendar Trigger	Detect event start
Process Data	Set / Function	Filter or format event info
Send Notification	Email / Slack / Twilio	Remind attendee or team

Key Takeaways

- Calendars can serve as both **triggers** and **targets** in workflows.
- Use them to ensure **timely notifications**, **event tracking**, and **reminder automation**.
- Combine with external services for full scheduling pipelines.

6.6 Social Media Platforms: X (Twitter), LinkedIn, Facebook

Social media automation is essential for marketing, brand engagement, and content distribution. n8n allows integration with platforms like **X (Twitter)**, **LinkedIn**, and **Facebook** to post updates, schedule content, or react to social triggers.

Learning Objectives

- Automatically post content to social platforms.
- Fetch engagement data and respond to events.
- Schedule campaigns and monitor hashtags or mentions.

Comparison Table: Social Media Integration

Platform	Authentication	Supported Actions	Limitations
X (Twitter)	OAuth1.0a / 2.0	Post tweet, read mentions, DM	Strict API limits and paid access tiers
LinkedIn	OAuth2	Share content, read profiles	Business API approval needed
Facebook	OAuth2	Post to page, fetch insights	Requires Facebook App + Page token

Flowchart: Scheduled Social Posting

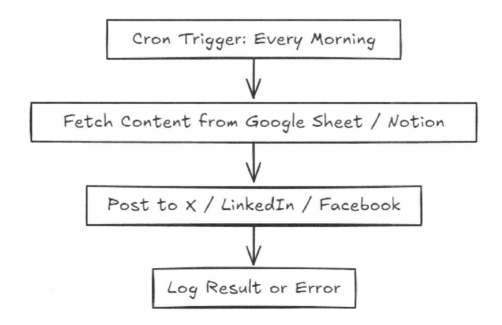

Step-by-Step: Automating Social Posts

1. **Trigger** workflow via Cron or form submission.
2. **Pull post content** from CMS, Google Sheets, or database.
3. **Send content** to social platform using respective nodes.
4. **Log post details** or response for analytics.

Example Table: Post Content Mapping

Platform	Content Source	Node Used	Sample Action
X	Google Sheet (Row)	X Node (Tweet)	Post Tweet: $json["text"]
LinkedIn	Notion Database	LinkedIn Node	Create Share Update
Facebook	Airtable or Custom Content	Facebook Page Node	Publish Page Post

Monitoring Engagement (Optional Workflows)

- **X Mentions Trigger** → Respond with a predefined message.
- **LinkedIn Post Stats** → Log impressions and likes weekly.
- **Facebook Comments Fetch** → Auto-log to CRM or Notion.

Key Takeaways

- n8n can automate **multi-platform content publishing**.
- You can create **scheduled posts, event-based responses**, and **engagement analytics**.
- Ensure proper API credentials and permissions before integrating.

Chapter 7: Developer Tools, Data Services & E-commerce

Chapter Objectives

- Understand how to automate processes with developer tools such as GitHub, GitLab, and CI/CD pipelines.
- Explore how to automate interactions with databases, APIs, and cloud services.
- Learn to create and manage e-commerce automation workflows for platforms like Stripe, PayPal, and Shopify.

7.1 GitHub, GitLab, CI/CD Automation

Developer platforms like GitHub and GitLab are central to modern software development. With n8n, you can automate continuous integration (CI), notifications, and repository maintenance. This section also covers how to use n8n in CI/CD pipelines.

Learning Objectives

- Automate Git-based workflows: pull requests, issues, commits.
- Integrate CI/CD processes with n8n.
- Improve dev team productivity with notifications and actions.

Workflow Flowchart: Auto-Notify on Pull Request

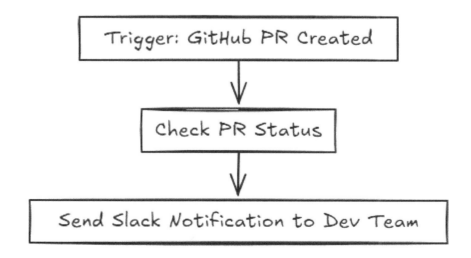

Git Platform Capabilities

Platform	Supported Triggers	Common Actions	Authentication
GitHub	Webhook (PR, push, issues, etc.)	Create issues, read commits, manage repos	Personal Access Token
GitLab	Webhook (pipeline, merge req.)	Trigger pipelines, manage repos	OAuth2 / Access Token

Example Use Cases

- **Slack Alerts** on pull request or merge.
- **Trigger Jenkins or CI builds** from commits.
- **Create GitHub Issues** automatically from errors in production logs.

CI/CD Automation Table

Event	Trigger Node	Action Node	Purpose
Code Push to Branch	GitHub Webhook	HTTP to Jenkins	Trigger CI pipeline
PR Opened	GitLab Webhook	Slack / Email	Notify reviewers
Deployment Complete	Jenkins Webhook	GitHub Issue	Log post-deployment tasks automatically

Key Takeaways

- Git-based automation with n8n enhances collaboration and deployment speed.
- Combine webhooks with notifications and HTTP requests to external CI tools.
- Handle pre-deploy and post-deploy tasks with n8n logic nodes.

7.2 Stripe, PayPal, Shopify

E-commerce automation with Stripe, PayPal, and Shopify enables streamlined order processing, payment management, and customer service. n8n can connect these services to CRMs, ERPs, and marketing platforms.

Learning Objectives

- Automate customer notifications and order tracking.
- Manage payment confirmations and refunds.
- Sync transactions with spreadsheets, accounting software, or databases.

Flowchart: New Order Processing

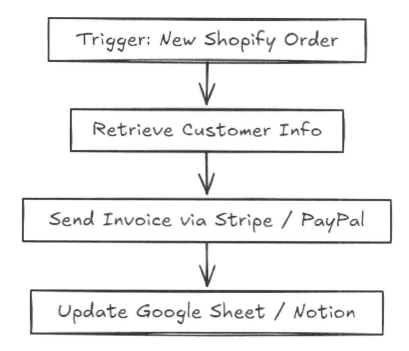

E-commerce Platform Capabilities

Platform	Triggers Available	Supported Actions	Authentication
Stripe	Payment received, refund	Create charge, issue refund, fetch invoices	API Key

PayPal	Webhooks via IPN	Process payment, refund, check status	OAuth2
Shopify	New order, product added	Get order, update inventory, manage customer	Private App Access

Use Case Examples

- **Stripe payment trigger** → Send thank-you email.
- **New Shopify order** → Update Airtable and send to fulfillment center.
- **Refund request via PayPal** → Notify support and log refund.

Automation Table: E-Commerce Integration

Task	Node(s) Used	Action
Send invoice email	Stripe + Email	On payment success, send confirmation
Log new order	Shopify + Google Sheet	Store order info for reports
Handle refund	PayPal + Slack	Notify support and tag refund in CRM

Key Takeaways

- Connect e-commerce tools to automate the **purchase-to-delivery** process.
- Ensure all data (orders, payments, refunds) are logged and synced across systems.
- Automate customer communication for smoother operations.

7.3 Databases: MySQL, PostgreSQL, MongoDB

n8n supports direct integration with popular databases, allowing you to read, write, and update data as part of your workflows. This empowers backend automation, report generation, and real-time analytics.

Learning Objectives

- Connect and authenticate with MySQL, PostgreSQL, and MongoDB.
- Perform read/write/update/delete operations from workflows.
- Use query results in downstream workflow steps.

Flowchart: Query and Report Generation

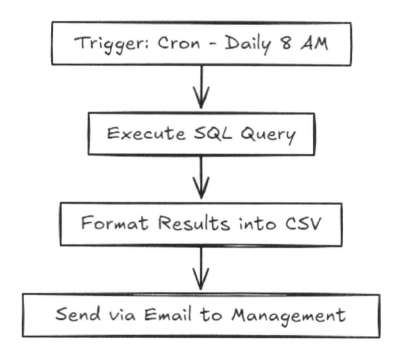

Database Node Capabilities Table

Database	Node Name	Authentication	Supported Operations
MySQL	MySQL	Host + User	SELECT, INSERT, UPDATE, DELETE

PostgreSQL	PostgreSQL	Host + User	SELECT, INSERT, UPDATE, DELETE
MongoDB	MongoDB	URI String	find, insertOne, updateOne, deleteOne

Example Use Cases

- Sync user data from an API into a PostgreSQL database.
- Run scheduled queries to generate performance metrics.
- Monitor database changes and trigger alerts or backups.

SQL Query Template Example (PostgreSQL)

```
SELECT user_id, last_login

FROM users

WHERE last_login < NOW() - INTERVAL '30 days';
```

Key Takeaways

- Use n8n's database nodes to centralize data from multiple sources.
- Combine data transformation logic with SQL and workflow logic.
- Ideal for reporting, backup, and system synchronization tasks.

7.4 REST, SOAP, and GraphQL APIs

APIs are at the heart of automation. n8n enables interaction with any service that exposes a REST, SOAP, or GraphQL API—even without a dedicated node—using the **HTTP Request** node.

Learning Objectives

- Use the HTTP Request node to integrate REST, SOAP, and GraphQL APIs.
- Build custom API interactions with headers, authentication, and payloads.
- Parse and use API responses in workflows.

Flowchart: REST API Integration Workflow

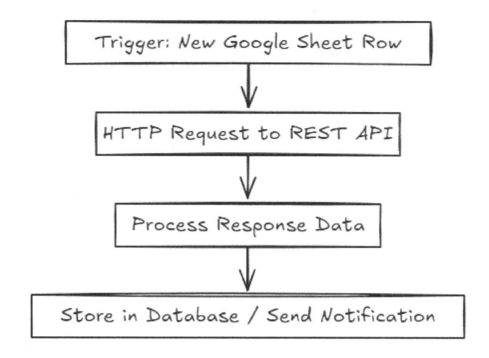

Comparison Table: API Protocols

Protocol	Typical Use Case	Format	Example Tool	Notes
REST	Most web APIs	JSON	GitHub API	Simple, widely used
SOAP	Enterprise systems (ERP)	XML	Salesforce SOAP	Requires WSDL, strict structure
GraphQL	Complex data queries	JSON (flexible)	GitHub GraphQL API	One request = multiple data points

Sample REST Request (JSON)

```json
{
  "method": "POST",
  "url": "https://api.example.com/users",
  "body": {
    "name": "Alice",
    "email": "alice@example.com"
  },
  "headers": {
    "Authorization": "Bearer YOUR_API_KEY"
  }
}
```

Key Takeaways

- REST is ideal for most standard APIs.
- SOAP is still used in legacy/enterprise systems—n8n can handle it with XML payloads.
- GraphQL enables complex querying with a single request.

7.5 File Storage: Dropbox, GDrive, S3, FTP

Automating file management tasks—such as uploads, backups, and file organization—is a powerful capability of n8n. Integrations with file storage providers like Dropbox, Google Drive, Amazon S3, and FTP servers allow seamless movement of data.

Learning Objectives

- Upload and download files from cloud storage or FTP using n8n nodes.
- Automate file backup, conversion, or notification workflows.
- Monitor directories or storage buckets for new files.

Flowchart: Upload File from Email to Dropbox

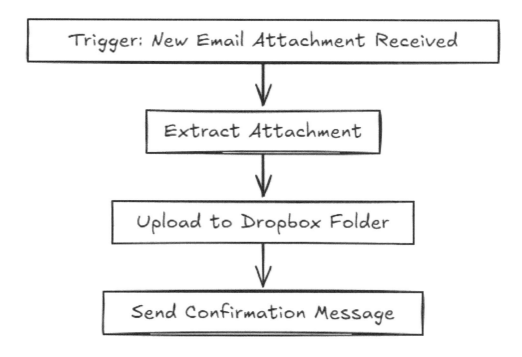

File Storage Integration Table

Storage Type	Node Name	Use Case	Notes
Dropbox	Dropbox	Backing up or sharing documents	Auth via OAuth2, supports folders/files
Google Drive	Google Drive	Syncing files across apps	Can search, upload, delete, move files
S3	Amazon S3	Static site hosting, backups	Requires access key/secret, supports ACL

FTP	FTP	Legacy file transfer automation	Use for private server file access

Example Use Case

Backup all new Airtable-generated PDF invoices daily to an S3 bucket and notify the finance team on Slack.

Sample File Upload Step (S3)

```
{

  "method": "PUT",

  "url": "https://mybucket.s3.amazonaws.com/invoice123.pdf",

  "headers": {

    "Content-Type": "application/pdf",

    "x-amz-acl": "private"

  },

  "body": "<BINARY FILE>"

}
```

Key Takeaways

- Use storage integrations for automated file processing workflows.
- Combine with logic nodes to build smart, organized backups.
- FTP still serves useful roles in older infrastructure or internal systems.

7.6 RSS, Webhooks, and Web Scraping

Automating information retrieval and event response is a major strength of n8n. You can track RSS feeds for content updates, use webhooks for real-time input, and perform lightweight web scraping.

Learning Objectives

- Monitor RSS feeds and send content updates to email or chat tools.

- Capture external events using Webhook triggers.
- Scrape data from websites using HTTP + HTML Extract nodes.

Flowchart: Monitor RSS Feed and Tweet Updates

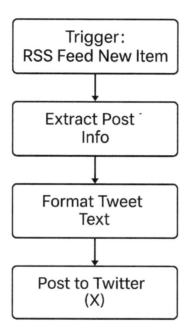

Integration Feature Table

Tool	Node Used	Key Use Case	Notes
RSS	RSS Feed Read	Automate blog/news monitoring	Supports filtering by keywords
Webhooks	Webhook	Listen for incoming HTTP events	Fully customizable payload, used in many flows

Web Scraping	HTTP + HTML	Extract prices, metadata, etc.	Requires understanding of HTML/CSS selectors

Sample HTML Extract (Scraping Example)

```
{

  "node": "HTML Extract",

  "selectors": {

   "title": "h1.article-title",

   "price": ".product-price"

  }

}
```

Key Takeaways

- RSS and scraping let you automate content tracking.
- Webhooks are essential for integrating with external systems in real-time.
- Combine these tools with logic and notifications to create intelligent workflows.

Chapter 8: Automation with AI and LLMs

Chapter Objectives

- Learn how to integrate AI and LLMs like ChatGPT and Claude into n8n workflows.
- Automate tasks like summarizing emails, generating content, and performing sentiment analysis.
- Leverage AI for smarter decision-making and intelligent process automation.
- Understand the practical uses of AI in automation to enhance your workflows.

8.1 Integrating OpenAI, ChatGPT, Claude

n8n enables integration with leading AI platforms like OpenAI (ChatGPT), Anthropic (Claude), and other LLM providers. These integrations allow users to inject natural language processing, summarization, classification, and content generation directly into automated workflows.

Learning Objectives

- Connect to OpenAI, Claude, and other LLMs via API.
- Send prompts and receive AI-generated responses in workflows.
- Use AI to enhance decision-making, summarization, and dynamic content creation.

Flowchart: AI-Powered Workflow with OpenAI

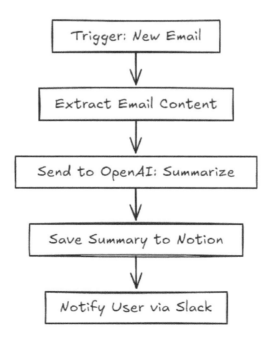

AI Integration Comparison Table

Provider	Node/API Used	Primary Use Cases	Authentication	Notes
OpenAI	HTTP Request	Text generation, summaries, Q&A	API Key	Supports GPT-3.5, GPT-4
Claude	HTTP Request	Safer/controlled language generation	API Key	Best for sensitive/controlled use
Cohere	HTTP Request	Embeddings, classification	API Key	Great for semantic search
HuggingFace	HTTP/Custom	Open-source LLMs	API Key	Offers hosted transformers and NLP models

Sample HTTP Request to OpenAI

```json
{
  "method": "POST",
  "url": "https://api.openai.com/v1/chat/completions",
  "headers": {
    "Authorization": "Bearer YOUR_API_KEY",
    "Content-Type": "application/json"
  },
  "body": {
    "model": "gpt-4",
    "messages": [
      { "role": "system", "content": "You are a helpful assistant." },
      { "role": "user", "content": "Summarize this email..." }
    ]
  }
}
```

Key Takeaways

- You can access cutting-edge AI directly within workflows using HTTP Request nodes.
- AI is best used for tasks requiring language understanding or generation.
- Combine AI output with conditional logic and integrations for intelligent automation.

8.2 AI-Powered Email and Text Summaries

Automated text summarization is one of the most impactful AI use cases. Using n8n, you can parse long emails, messages, or documents and summarize them for faster decision-making or alerts.

Learning Objectives

- Create workflows that detect long text input and generate summaries.

- Use summaries for automated notifications, documentation, or categorization.
- Apply summarization in email, CRM, and knowledge base contexts.

Flowchart: Summarize Email with AI and Send Digest

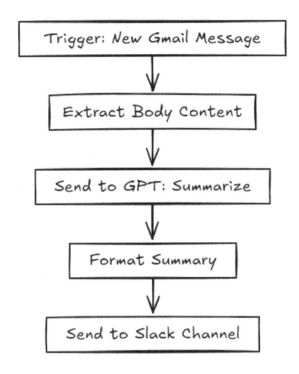

Use Case Table

Scenario	AI Integration Use	Benefit
Long-form Email Review	Summarize and extract key points	Saves time, improves decision speed
Ticketing System Summaries	Condense support messages	Improves triage and support quality
CRM Note Compilation	Aggregate customer notes	Better insights and history

Meeting Transcript Summarizer	Generate meeting notes	Automates documentation

Step-by-Step Guide: AI Email Digest Bot

1. **Trigger:** Gmail node triggers on new email.
2. **Extract:** Use Set or HTML Extract to pull content.
3. **Send:** Use HTTP Request to OpenAI or Claude with a summarization prompt.
4. **Format:** Use Function or Set node to style the output.
5. **Output:** Send summary to Slack or store in Notion.

Prompt Design Tip

Make your AI prompts specific and focused:

"Summarize the following customer email in 3 bullet points, focusing on pain points and requested features."

Key Takeaways

- Text summarization is a powerful automation booster.
- Use AI to extract insights from unstructured data.
- Carefully crafted prompts yield better summarization results.

8.3 Automating Content Generation

AI-powered content generation allows you to create blog posts, product descriptions, emails, reports, and more—automatically. With n8n and LLM APIs like OpenAI and Claude, you can automate content production pipelines at scale.

Learning Objectives

- Automatically generate text content using LLMs in workflows.
- Design prompts for various content types (emails, blogs, ads).
- Use n8n nodes to store, format, and distribute generated content.

Flowchart: Content Generation Workflow

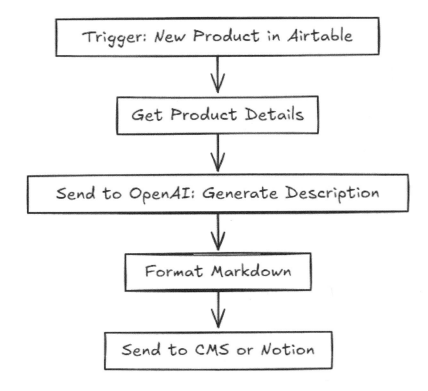

Content Generation Use Case Table

Use Case	Trigger Node	AI Prompt Type	Output Destination
Blog Article Creation	Cron Schedule	Long-form content	CMS or Google Docs
Product Descriptions	Airtable/Webhook	SEO-optimized product summary	Shopify/CSV export
Marketing Emails	Manual Trigger	Promotional copy	Mailchimp or Gmail
Social Media Posts	RSS or Cron	Engaging 1-2 sentence summary	Buffer or LinkedIn API

Prompt Engineering Example

Write a 100-word product description for a {product_name}, highlighting key features and benefits. Use a friendly and persuasive tone.

Hands-On Workflow Steps

1. **Trigger**: Use Airtable trigger for new product entry.
2. **Extract**: Use Set node to format product details.
3. **Generate**: Use HTTP Request to OpenAI with a prompt.
4. **Format**: Use Markdown or HTML node for styling.
5. **Output**: Send to CMS or export to a spreadsheet.

Key Takeaways

- AI can accelerate content creation, reduce human error, and maintain consistency.
- Designing the right prompts is crucial to generating useful content.
- You can fully automate content pipelines with no-code tools and LLMs.

8.4 Smart Decision-Making with AI

AI is not only for generating content—it can also help make intelligent decisions. You can use LLMs to analyze input, assess sentiment, prioritize tickets, or suggest next steps based on logic embedded in prompts.

Learning Objectives

- Use AI to enhance business logic in workflows.
- Analyze customer data and provide intelligent responses.
- Build smart decision trees using dynamic AI output.

Flowchart: AI-Based Decision Making Workflow

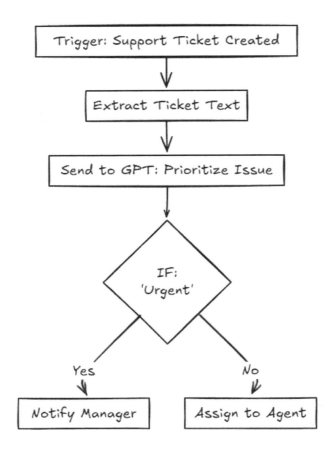

Example Prompts for Decision Making

Classify this support ticket as "Urgent", "High", "Normal", or "Low" priority. Just return one of those labels.

Based on the email content below, should we escalate this to a human agent? Answer "Yes" or "No".

Use Case Table

Scenario	AI Role	Output Action
Ticket Escalation	Assess urgency	Send to support or manager

Lead Qualification	Evaluate form data	Score or label
Customer Sentiment Analysis	Analyze tone	Route or flag messages
Email Response Decision	Generate reply suggestions	Human review or auto-send

Tips for Smart Logic Integration

- Use **Function** nodes to convert AI responses into routeable logic.
- Combine with **IF** and **Switch** nodes to split flow based on AI classification.
- Use **error handling** to catch ambiguous AI output.

Key Takeaways

- LLMs can classify, decide, and guide automation paths intelligently.
- Integrate smart logic using prompt-based classification or prioritization.
- Always validate and refine prompts to ensure consistent output.

8.5 Sentiment Analysis and Classification

Sentiment analysis allows your workflows to understand the tone and emotion behind messages, feedback, or reviews. Classification helps group content by type, intent, or category. Together, these capabilities can transform unstructured text into actionable insight using n8n and LLMs or third-party NLP APIs.

Learning Objectives

- Understand how to perform sentiment analysis using AI within n8n.
- Classify text into categories (e.g., complaint, praise, inquiry).
- Automate routing or responses based on sentiment or classification.

Flowchart: Sentiment Analysis in Workflow Automation

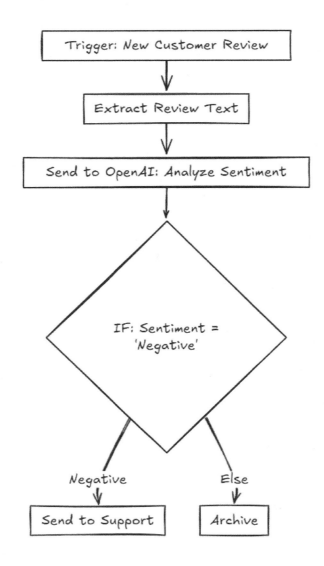

Use Case Table

Scenario	Input Source	Analysis Type	Automated Action
Customer Support Feedback	Email or Form	Sentiment + Intent	Escalate or auto-respond

Product Reviews	E-commerce platform	Sentiment	Highlight positive/flag negative
Social Media Mentions	Twitter, Facebook	Sentiment + Category	Route to marketing or support
Employee Survey Analysis	Internal form	Emotion Classification	HR follow-up or trend reporting

Sample Prompts for Sentiment and Classification

Classify the sentiment of the following message as "Positive", "Neutral", or "Negative":

"{customer_feedback}"

Determine the intent of this message: "Complaint", "Question", "Praise", or "Other".

"{message_text}"

Based on this review, what emotions are being expressed? Provide a one-word answer.

Workflow Example: Classify Support Ticket Type

1. **Trigger**: New ticket received via webhook.
2. **Set Node**: Extract ticket message.
3. **HTTP Request**: Send message to OpenAI/Claude for classification.
4. **IF Node**: Split based on result — e.g., "Complaint" → escalate, "Question" → autoresponder.
5. **Log Result**: Save classification in Airtable/Google Sheets.

Table: Sentiment Values and Routing Actions

Sentiment	Action
Positive	Tag as "Praise", archive

Neutral	Monitor, no escalation
Negative	Escalate to human support

Tips for Effective AI-Based Text Analysis

- Use **short, precise prompts** to reduce ambiguity.
- Add guardrails in workflows for unexpected or blank results.
- Combine classification with **metadata** (e.g., time, source) for deeper automation.

Key Takeaways

- Sentiment and classification let you derive insight from unstructured text.
- Automate decisions like escalation, routing, and response generation based on sentiment.
- Text analysis improves responsiveness, customer satisfaction, and internal efficiency.

Chapter 9: Advanced Automation Techniques

Chapter Objectives

- Learn advanced automation techniques for optimizing workflows and enhancing performance.
- Dive into techniques such as pagination, rate limiting, and handling long-running workflows.
- Understand how to securely manage API tokens and configure long-running workflows.
- Master the tools and techniques for creating more complex and scalable automations.

9.1 JavaScript for Custom Logic

While n8n is a no-code tool, it also supports JavaScript for users who want to go beyond the built-in capabilities. This chapter focuses on how to leverage the **Function** and **FunctionItem** nodes to write JavaScript code that transforms data, adds logic, and creates custom automation behavior.

Learning Objectives

- Understand the difference between **Function** and **FunctionItem** nodes.
- Learn how to use JavaScript to manipulate data within a workflow.
- Apply advanced logic not possible with visual nodes alone.

Flowchart: Where JavaScript Fits in a Workflow

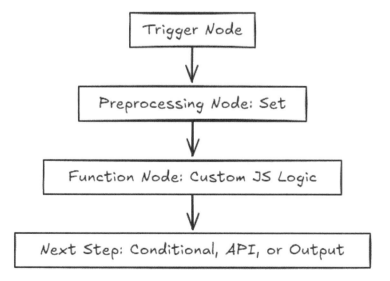

Function vs. FunctionItem: Comparison Table

Feature	Function Node	FunctionItem Node
Processes	Entire array of items	Each item individually
Access to context	Full items array and metadata	Only current item (item.json, etc.)
Use Case	Bulk data manipulation, merging, filtering	Per-record transformation or value mapping

Example 1: Calculating Total Price with Tax

```
// FunctionItem Node

const taxRate = 0.075;

item.total = item.price + item.price * taxRate;

return item;
```

Example 2: Filtering Items by Condition

```
// Function Node

return items.filter(item => item.json.amount > 100);
```

Use Cases for JavaScript in n8n

Use Case	Node Type	Description
Data Transformation	FunctionItem	Modify object structure or values
Custom Filtering	Function	Remove items based on complex logic
Dynamic API Parameters	Function	Build dynamic query strings or request bodies
Conditional Routing (Advanced)	Function	Replace nested IF chains with JS logic
Error Formatting or Cleanup	FunctionItem	Clean up dirty or inconsistent data

Common Objects in JavaScript Nodes

Object	Purpose
item	The current input item in FunctionItem node
items	All input items in Function node
item.json	The main data payload
item.binary	Any attached binary data
this.helpers	Access to helper functions

Key Takeaways

- JavaScript in n8n unlocks flexible, powerful logic.
- Use **FunctionItem** for record-level changes and **Function** for full-array operations.
- Clean, well-commented code ensures maintainability and scalability.

9.2 Pagination, Rate Limiting, and Throttling

Many APIs enforce constraints such as **pagination**, **rate limits**, and **throttling**. To ensure smooth automation, it's essential to design workflows that comply with these limits. This section explores how to handle these scenarios using n8n's built-in capabilities and scripting.

Learning Objectives

- Understand how to work with paginated API responses.
- Learn how to avoid exceeding API rate limits.
- Implement throttling strategies in your workflows.

Flowchart: Handling API Pagination and Rate Limits

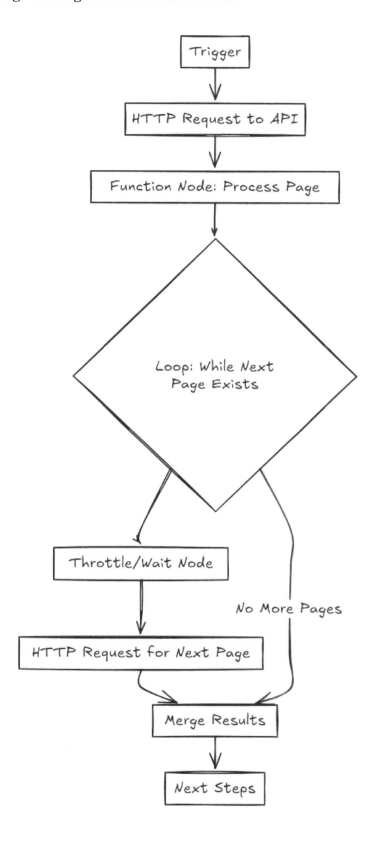

Pagination Strategies

Type	Description	Example Usage
Offset-based	Use offset and limit query params	?offset=0&limit=100
Cursor-based	Use a nextPageToken or cursor in the response	?cursor=XYZ123
Page-based	Use page and per_page or similar	?page=2&per_page=50

Step-by-Step: Offset-Based Pagination Example

1. **Initial Request:**
   o Use HTTP node with ?offset=0&limit=100.
2. **Loop With While or Function Node:**
   o Check response length or existence of next page.
3. **Update Offset:**
   o Add 100 to the offset value for the next request.
4. **Merge Results:**
   o Use Merge node or append in Function node.

Handling Rate Limits

API Behavior	Strategy	n8n Node
429 Too Many Requests	Use **Wait** node based on Retry-After	Wait
X requests per minute	Throttle using set intervals	Wait / Delay
Burst prevention	Add delays between requests	Function + Wait

Throttle Timing: Table of Examples

API Limit	Throttle Rule
60 requests/minute	1 request every 1 second
10 requests/second	1 request every 100ms
500/day	Time-based scheduler or monitor

Best Practices

- Always read API documentation to know the limit type.
- Check headers like X-RateLimit-Remaining, Retry-After.
- Use **Set**, **Wait**, and **Function** nodes to control timing.

Example: Adding Delay Between Requests

```
// Use Wait node with fixed delay

{

 "parameters": {

  "value": 1000,

  "unit": "ms"

 }

}
```

Key Takeaways

- Pagination and rate-limiting must be handled explicitly in workflows.
- Use **loops** and **delay nodes** to paginate and throttle.
- Always monitor API responses to adapt to changing limits.

9.3 API Token Rotation

API tokens are commonly used for authenticating and authorizing API requests. Over time, these tokens may expire or need to be rotated for security reasons. In this section, we will explore how to handle **API token rotation** in n8n, ensuring continuous access to services without interruptions.

Learning Objectives

- Understand the need for API token rotation.
- Learn how to manage expired tokens in n8n workflows.
- Implement token refresh logic using HTTP requests and expressions.

Flowchart: API Token Rotation Process

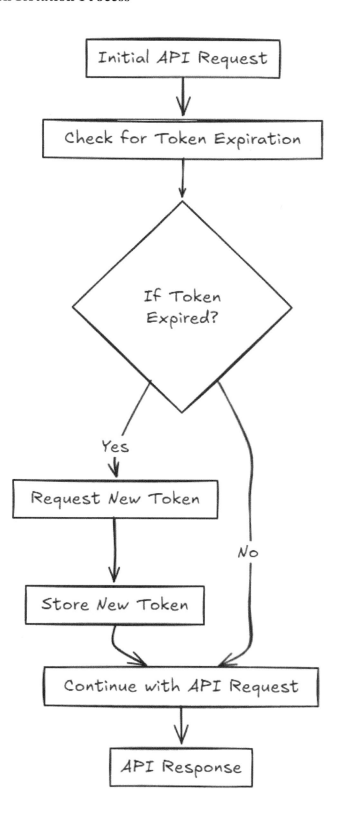

When to Use API Token Rotation

- **Token Expiry**: Tokens typically expire after a set period. They need to be refreshed to continue making requests.
- **Security Protocol**: Regularly rotating tokens improves security by reducing the risk of token misuse.

Common Methods of API Token Rotation

Method	Description	Example
Refresh Tokens	Use a refresh token to obtain a new access token.	POST /oauth/token with refresh_token
Re-authenticate	Re-authenticate the user to obtain a new access token.	Use username/password to get a new token
Static Rotation	Manually rotate the token and update it in the workflow.	Store token in n8n's environment variables

Step-by-Step: Handling Token Expiration

1. **Check Token Expiry**: Determine if the token has expired by checking the API response status code (e.g., 401 Unauthorized).
2. **Request New Token**: If expired, make a request to the API's token endpoint with a valid refresh token.
3. **Update Token in Workflow**: Store the new token using the **Set** or **Set Multiple** node.
4. **Continue Request**: Once the token is refreshed, retry the original API request with the new token.

Example: Using a Refresh Token for Rotation

```
{
"method": "POST",

"url": "https://api.example.com/oauth/token",
```

```
"json": {

 "grant_type": "refresh_token",

 "refresh_token": "your_refresh_token"

 }

}
```

Best Practices for API Token Rotation

- Use **environment variables** to store API tokens securely.
- Implement error handling for expired tokens within workflows.
- Rotate tokens based on the expiration period, and set up monitoring to prevent service interruptions.
- **Set a retry logic** to handle token refresh failures gracefully.

Key Takeaways

- Regularly rotating API tokens enhances security and reliability.
- You can automate token refresh by implementing HTTP requests within your workflows.
- Always ensure that tokens are securely stored using environment variables or encrypted storage.

9.4 Long-Running Workflows and Timeouts

Long-running workflows, such as those involving large data processing or external API calls that take a long time to respond, can face challenges related to **timeouts** and **execution limits**. This section explores how to manage and optimize long-running workflows in n8n to prevent failures and ensure smooth operation.

Learning Objectives

- Understand the limitations of long-running workflows.
- Learn how to prevent timeouts during API calls and long tasks.
- Implement strategies to handle tasks that run for extended periods.

Flowchart: Handling Long-Running Workflows

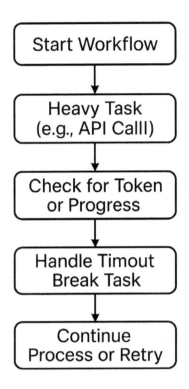

Challenges with Long-Running Workflows

Challenge	Impact	Solution
Timeout	n8n or external APIs may timeout, causing workflow failure.	Increase timeout settings or use retries.
Resource Usage	Long workflows may consume excessive server resources.	Break tasks into smaller sub-workflows.
State Management	Workflow state may be lost in case of failures.	Use database or external storage for state.

Strategies for Handling Long-Running Workflows

1. Increase Timeout Settings

Many APIs and nodes in n8n have configurable timeout settings. Increase these settings if you know the workflow will take a long time to complete.

For HTTP requests:

```
{

  "timeout": 60000  // Set timeout to 60 seconds

}
```

2. Use Wait or Delay Nodes

For tasks that need to run over extended periods, consider splitting the task into smaller parts and using **Wait** or **Delay** nodes to pause between steps.

Example using **Wait Node**:

```
{

 "parameters": {

  "value": 300000,  // 5-minute wait

  "unit": "ms"

 }

}
```

3. Use External Storage for State Management

For workflows that might be interrupted, store the state of the process (e.g., current step, partial results) in a database or a file storage service (e.g., Google Sheets, MySQL).

Handling API Timeouts and Retrying

Strategy	Description	Example
Retry on Failure	Implement retries in case of a timeout or failure.	Use **Retry** node to retry on failure.
Progress Indicators	Use external logging or storage to track progress.	Store current progress in a database.

Key Takeaways

- For long-running workflows, carefully manage timeouts and retries.
- Break workflows into smaller, manageable chunks and use external state management for persistence.
- Use **Wait**, **Delay**, and **Retry** nodes to optimize workflow performance and prevent failures.

9.5 External Service Syncing (2-Way Automation)

Two-way automation, or **bi-directional syncing**, involves keeping data consistent between two services or systems—automatically updating one when changes occur in the other. This is crucial for use cases like syncing CRM records, calendar events, or task management tools. In this section, you'll learn how to implement reliable and efficient two-way syncing in **n8n**.

Learning Objectives

- Understand the concept and challenges of two-way automation.
- Learn how to detect and handle changes across multiple systems.
- Build a robust two-way sync with n8n using triggers, polling, and version control.

What Is 2-Way Syncing?

Two-way syncing ensures that changes made in **Service A** are reflected in **Service B**, and vice versa, without data conflicts or duplication.

Flowchart: 2-Way Syncing Logic

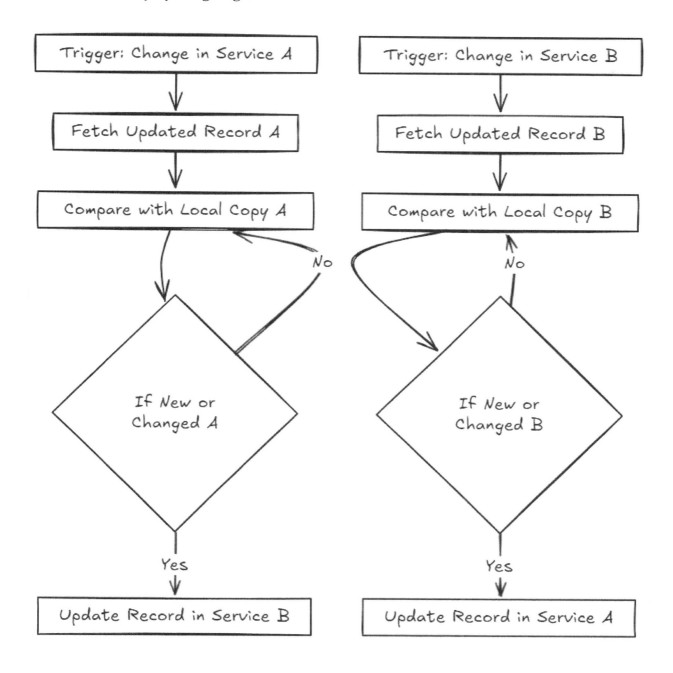

Key Components in n8n

Component	Purpose
Trigger Node	Detects changes in either service (e.g., webhook, polling).
HTTP Request / SaaS Node	Sends/receives data to/from external service.
Set / Merge / IF Node	Determines whether data has changed.
Database / Static Data	Stores last synced state to avoid duplicates.

Challenges in 2-Way Syncing

Challenge	Solution
Duplication	Use unique IDs and timestamp checks to prevent reprocessing same records.
Data Conflicts	Use timestamps or version fields to resolve the most recent change.
Infinite Loops	Tag synced records to avoid triggering sync loops.
Latency & Delays	Schedule periodic syncs or implement queuing logic.

Example Use Case: Notion ↔ Trello Task Sync

1. **Detect New or Updated Tasks in Notion**
   ○ Use a webhook or scheduled poll to check for updates.
2. **Compare Last Synced Data**
   ○ Retrieve last known state from Airtable, Redis, or n8n static data.
3. **Update Trello**
   ○ If changed, push the update to Trello.
4. **Vice Versa** (Trello → Notion)
   ○ Repeat the logic to check Trello for changes and push updates to Notion.

Best Practices

- **Tag Synced Items**: Add metadata like synced: true to track what has already been handled.
- **Use Timestamps**: Compare updated_at fields to decide which side holds the latest version.
- **Error Handling**: Log failed updates and retry automatically to ensure reliability.
- **Avoid Loops**: Include logic to skip updates triggered by sync itself.

Key Takeaways

- Two-way syncing ensures data consistency between systems but requires thoughtful logic to avoid loops and conflicts.
- Use n8n nodes like **IF, Set, Webhook**, and **HTTP Request** to build condition-driven sync logic.
- Store previous state and track changes for reliable and efficient automation.

Chapter 10: Credentials and Security

Chapter Objectives

- Understand the importance of securely managing credentials and secrets in n8n workflows
- Learn how to handle API keys, OAuth2 tokens, and other sensitive data
- Explore methods to secure credentials and prevent unauthorized access
- Learn how to configure environment-specific settings and use secret managers for additional security

---

10.1 Managing API Keys, Tokens, OAuth2

APIs are the backbone of n8n workflows, and securing access to them requires proper **authentication mechanisms**. This section explains how to manage **API keys, OAuth2 tokens**, and **other credentials** within n8n securely and efficiently.

Learning Objectives

- Understand the different types of API authentication methods.
- Learn how to use n8n's credential management system.
- Configure OAuth2 for dynamic and secure integrations.

Types of Authentication in n8n

Method	Description	Example Use Cases
API Key	Static key included in headers or URL	Mailgun, SendGrid
Basic Auth	Username and password (Base64 encoded)	Simple HTTP APIs

OAuth2	Secure token-based method with scopes and refresh	Google, Slack, Microsoft Graph
Bearer Token	Single-use or reusable token in headers	OpenAI, Dropbox

Flowchart: Credential Use in Workflow

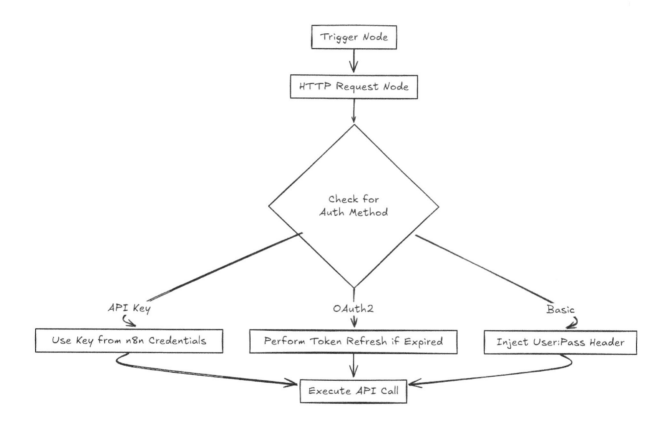

n8n Credential Manager

The **Credential Manager** allows you to store and reuse sensitive data like API keys and OAuth tokens without hardcoding them in nodes.

Feature	Description
Encryption	All credentials are encrypted on disk
Reusability	Credentials can be used across multiple workflows
Credential Types	Built-in types (Google, Slack) or custom-defined
Token Refresh Support	Automatic OAuth2 refresh based on expiry time

How to Add a New Credential in n8n

Step-by-step:

1. Go to **Credentials** in the left-hand menu.
2. Click **"New Credential"** and select a service (e.g., Slack, Google Sheets).
3. Fill in the required fields:
   - For API Key: Enter the static key.
   - For OAuth2: Provide Client ID, Client Secret, and redirect URIs.
4. Click **Connect** (for OAuth2) or **Save**.
5. Use this credential in any node that supports authentication.

Best Practices

- **Never hardcode sensitive data** in nodes—always use the credential manager.
- Use **separate credentials per environment** (e.g., dev, staging, prod).
- Regularly **rotate API keys** and review token expiration policies.

- For OAuth2: Always configure the **refresh token flow** to prevent broken sessions.

Key Takeaways

- Credentials are securely stored and managed in n8n's built-in Credential Manager.
- Always choose the most secure and appropriate method (OAuth2 > API Key > Basic Auth).
- Secure credentials reduce the risk of leaks and simplify integration management.

10.2 Securing Credentials and Secrets

As automation workflows handle sensitive data, securing credentials is crucial to avoid leaks, unauthorized access, or compliance violations. This section outlines **how n8n secures secrets**, how you can enhance that security, and best practices for keeping workflows safe.

Learning Objectives

- Understand how n8n encrypts and stores credentials.
- Learn strategies for securely managing secrets.
- Implement credential access control and audit best practices.

Credential Storage and Encryption in n8n

Security Layer	Description
Encryption at Rest	All stored credentials are encrypted using AES encryption.
Encrypted Database	Credentials stored in SQLite/PostgreSQL are encrypted before being saved.
Environment Isolation	Each instance of n8n manages its own credential set.

Access-Controlled UI	Credentials are not visible in plaintext once saved in the UI.

Flowchart: Secure Credential Lifecycle in n8n

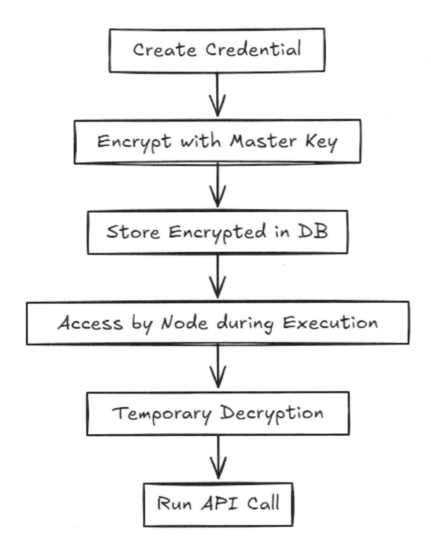

Security Best Practices

Best Practice	Description
Use .env for Secrets	Store credentials like N8N_ENCRYPTION_KEY in a .env file, not hardcoded
Protect the Encryption Key	Store N8N_ENCRYPTION_KEY securely—it's needed to decrypt all credentials
Limit User Access in n8n UI	Ensure only authorized users can create/edit credentials
Run n8n Behind Authentication	Always protect the n8n instance with user login and 2FA if possible
Use a Secrets Management System	Integrate with tools like HashiCorp Vault or AWS Secrets Manager if needed

Example .env Configuration File

```
# .env

N8N_ENCRYPTION_KEY=9a1b8f3a2c1d4e6g7h2j3k4l5m6n7o8p

N8N_BASIC_AUTH_USER=admin

N8N_BASIC_AUTH_PASSWORD=StrongPasswordHere
```

Key Takeaways

- n8n encrypts all credentials at rest, but you must secure your .env file and access permissions.
- Never expose credentials in workflow logic or code—use the Credential Manager.

- Implement access control and secure deployment to prevent leakage.

10.3 Environment-Specific Configurations

In production, staging, and development, different workflows may require different **credentials, APIs, and behaviors**. n8n supports environment-specific configuration using .env variables and modular design.

Learning Objectives

- Set up environment-specific values using environment variables.
- Switch credentials or nodes based on the environment.
- Isolate sensitive or experimental workflows.

Using Environment Variables

n8n reads configuration from a .env file or system-level environment settings.

Variable	Purpose
N8N_ENCRYPTION_KEY	Encrypt/decrypt credentials
N8N_BASIC_AUTH_USER	Basic auth username
N8N_BASIC_AUTH_PASSWORD	Basic auth password
NODE_ENV	Define environment: development, production
N8N_LOG_LEVEL	Controls logging verbosity

Flowchart: Workflow Execution Based on Environment

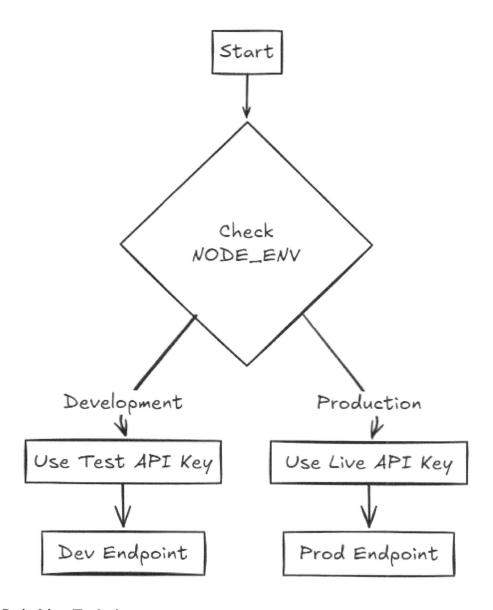

Dynamic Switching Techniques

1. **Use Set Node to Load Env Variables**:
   o Read process.env.CUSTOM_VAR in a Function or Set node.
2. **Store Conditional Logic**:
   o Add IF node to route based on environment.
3. **Credential Variants**:
   o Create separate credentials like Stripe_Dev and Stripe_Prod.

Best Practices for Managing Environments

Practice	Benefit
Separate Workspaces	Avoid mixing live and test data
Environment-specific Credentials	Prevent accidental usage of production data
Automated Deployment (CI/CD)	Ensure consistent deployment per environment
Audit Logs	Track credential usage by workflow and user

Key Takeaways

- Use .env and credential variants to isolate environments.
- Make workflows dynamic to switch APIs, keys, or nodes based on environment.
- Keep development secure and separate from production for safety and compliance.

10.4 Using .env Files and Secret Managers

Managing secrets securely is critical for any automation. n8n supports .env files for environment-specific secrets, and advanced users can integrate secret management tools like HashiCorp Vault, AWS Secrets Manager, and others.

Learning Objectives

- Configure .env files to store sensitive data.
- Understand secret manager integration options.
- Safely reference environment variables in workflows.

Using .env Files in n8n

.env files allow you to define environment variables that can be accessed by the system and within workflows.

Example .env File:

```
# n8n .env file

N8N_ENCRYPTION_KEY=supersecurekey123

STRIPE_API_KEY=sk_test_abc123

MAILGUN_API_KEY=key-xyz456

NODE_ENV=production
```

Place this file at the root of your n8n project directory.

Referencing Variables in Workflows

Use JavaScript expressions or Function nodes:

```
const stripeKey = $env.STRIPE_API_KEY;
```

Or in expression fields:

```
={{ $env.STRIPE_API_KEY }}
```

Flowchart: Secrets Usage Flow

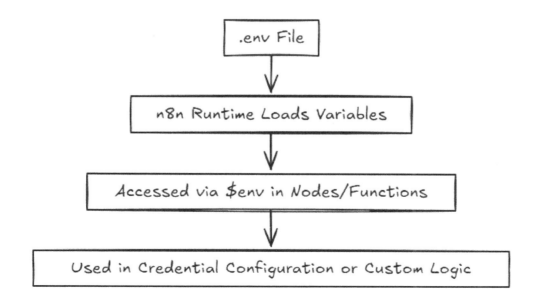

Using Secret Managers (Optional for Advanced Users)

Secret Manager	Integration Method	Advantages
HashiCorp Vault	Sidecar, CLI, or custom script	Centralized, versioned, access-controlled
AWS Secrets Manager	AWS CLI + shell export or Lambda fetch	Scalable, audit-logged, managed by AWS
Docker Secrets	Docker secrets mount to container files	Great for containerized n8n deployments

Best Practices for Secret Storage

- Never hardcode secrets in workflows.
- Restrict access to the .env file (chmod 600 .env).
- Use secret managers in production for high-security environments.

Key Takeaways

- .env files are simple and effective for managing secrets during development.
- Use $env to dynamically inject secrets into nodes.
- Advanced deployments benefit from secret managers for scale, security, and auditing.

10.5 Common Security Pitfalls to Avoid

Security mishaps often stem from avoidable mistakes. This section outlines the most common pitfalls and how to prevent them in n8n deployments.

Learning Objectives

- Recognize insecure practices in credential management.
- Avoid workflow design patterns that expose sensitive data.
- Learn prevention strategies for secure automations.

Table: Common Pitfalls and Solutions

Pitfall	Consequence	Prevention Strategy
Hardcoding credentials in workflows	Credentials can be leaked, reused, or abused	Use Credential Manager or .env variables
Sharing workflows with credentials	Sensitive info can be exposed	Export workflows **without** credentials
Weak encryption key	Easy for attackers to decrypt credentials	Use a **strong** N8N_ENCRYPTION_KEY
Public n8n instances without auth	Unauthorized access to all workflows	Enable Basic Auth or OAuth login
Insecure webhook exposure	Allows unwanted external triggers	Use secret URLs, IP whitelisting, or tokens
Lack of audit logs	No traceability on credential access	Enable server logging and user management
Single set of shared credentials	No control or isolation	Use role-based access and separate credentials

Checklist: Secure Automation Design

- Are all secrets stored in Credential Manager or .env?
- Is access to the n8n instance protected (auth, VPN, or firewall)?
- Are workflow exports scrubbed of sensitive data?
- Are audit logs enabled and stored securely?

- Are users limited by roles or permissions?

Key Takeaways

- Avoid hardcoded secrets and always review workflows before sharing or exporting.
- Implement strong encryption and secure .env access.
- Secure endpoints, limit user access, and track credential usage.

Chapter 11: Creating Custom Nodes

Chapter Objectives

- Understand the process of creating custom nodes in n8n
- Learn how to set up the development environment for node creation
- Explore how to write, debug, and test custom nodes
- Know how to share and publish custom nodes with the community

11.1 to Node Development

While n8n provides hundreds of built-in nodes, advanced users and developers may want to create **custom nodes** tailored to specific services or logic. This chapter introduces the fundamentals of n8n node development.

Learning Objectives

- Understand the anatomy of a custom node.
- Learn the lifecycle and purpose of each part of a node.
- Know when and why to create a custom node.

What Is a Custom Node?

A custom node is a reusable, pluggable unit built using **TypeScript** or **JavaScript** that extends n8n's core functionality, allowing integration with external services or custom business logic.

Use Cases for Custom Nodes

Use Case	Description
Proprietary API integration	Service is not supported by native n8n nodes
Encapsulation of business logic	Reuse complex logic across workflows

UI custom inputs	Provide specific input fields or drop-downs
Simplified team usage	Wrap logic in an easy-to-use node for others

Anatomy of a Node

A node file includes:

- **Name, display name, description**
- **Inputs/outputs**
- **Properties (user-configurable fields)**
- **Execution logic**

Flowchart: Node Development Lifecycle

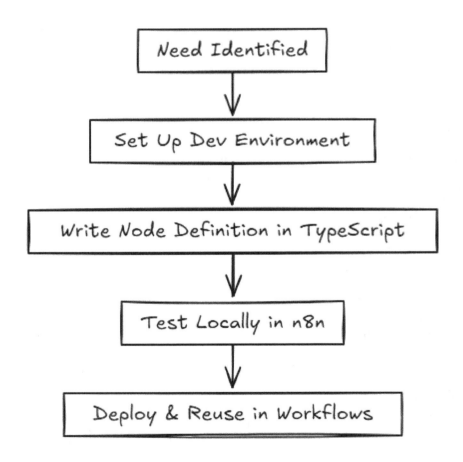

Key Takeaways

- Custom nodes expand n8n's flexibility beyond built-in capabilities.
- They're ideal for internal tools, proprietary systems, or reusable logic.
- You write them in TypeScript and plug them into the n8n runtime.

11.2 Setting Up the Dev Environment

Before creating a node, you need to prepare your local environment with the right tools, repositories, and configuration.

Learning Objectives

- Set up a development-ready n8n instance.
- Clone the source code and install dependencies.
- Run and test n8n locally.

Step-by-Step: Environment Setup

1. Prerequisites:

- Node.js (LTS version, e.g., 18+)
- Git
- Docker (optional)
- Yarn (preferred over npm)

2. Clone the n8n Repository

git clone https://github.com/n8n-io/n8n.git

cd n8n

3. Install Dependencies

yarn install

4. Run in Development Mode

yarn dev

This runs n8n in watch mode for fast development and testing.

Table: Key Folders in n8n Repository

Folder Path	Description
/packages/nodes-base	Built-in nodes; used as reference models
/packages/nodes-custom	Where your custom nodes can be added
/packages/cli	Main CLI logic to run n8n
/packages/editor-ui	Frontend editor for visual workflow design

n8n Dev Tips

- Use **hot reload** (yarn dev) to test changes without restarting.
- Create a **custom package** for your organization's internal nodes.
- Use the **example nodes** in nodes-base as templates.

Key Takeaways

- A local dev setup is essential for node development.
- Use the n8n monorepo and Yarn to streamline development.
- Structure your code based on existing nodes and best practices.

11.3 Writing and Debugging a Custom Node

Once the development environment is set up, you can begin writing your custom node. This section walks you through creating a basic node and debugging it in your local n8n instance.

Learning Objectives

- Understand the structure of a node definition file.
- Learn how to define inputs, outputs, and parameters.
- Debug and test your custom node effectively.

Step-by-Step: Writing a Custom Node

1. Create a New Node File

In /packages/nodes-custom/nodes/MyCustomNode/, create a new file:

MyCustomNode.node.ts

2. Define the Node Structure

Here's a basic example:

```typescript
import { INodeType, INodeTypeDescription, IExecuteFunctions } from 'n8n-workflow';

export class MyCustomNode implements INodeType {

  description: INodeTypeDescription = {

    displayName: 'My Custom Node',

    name: 'myCustomNode',

    group: ['transform'],

    version: 1,

    description: 'A simple custom node example',

    defaults: {

      name: 'MyCustomNode',

    },

    inputs: ['main'],

    outputs: ['main'],

    properties: [

      {

        displayName: 'Input Text',
```

```
      name: 'inputText',

      type: 'string',

      default: '',

      placeholder: 'Enter some text...',

     },

    ],

  };

  async execute(this: IExecuteFunctions) {

    const inputText = this.getNodeParameter('inputText', 0) as string;

    const result = `${inputText} - processed by MyCustomNode`;

    return [this.helpers.returnJsonArray([{ result }])];

  }

}
```

Debugging Tips

Method	Purpose
console.log()	Output values in terminal (Node process)
this.getNodeParameter()	Fetch user input from the node config
this.helpers.returnJsonArray()	Format output in the expected JSON format

Flowchart: Debug Cycle

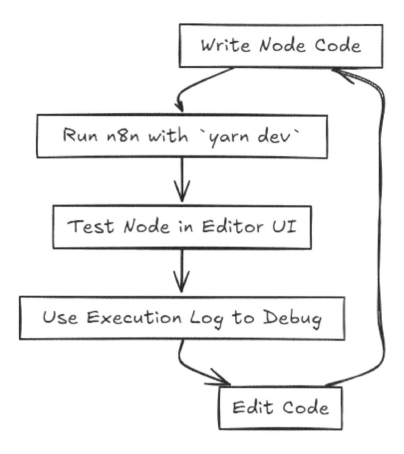

Common Errors & Fixes

Error	Solution
Node not found	Ensure the class is exported correctly
Missing parameters	Check for parameter names in getNodeParameter()
No output in execution	Ensure returnJsonArray() returns a valid array

Key Takeaways

- Node definition includes metadata, UI fields, and execution logic.
- Debug using logs and execution output in the editor.
- Test frequently using yarn dev for real-time feedback.

11.4 Community Node Sharing

n8n encourages the open sharing of custom nodes through its community ecosystem. This enables collaboration and extension of automation capabilities beyond the core product.

Learning Objectives

- Learn how to publish and distribute custom nodes.
- Understand best practices for documentation and versioning.
- Discover how to use and install community-contributed nodes.

Step-by-Step: Sharing a Node

1. Convert Your Node to a Package

Create a new directory in /packages/ and structure it as a standalone npm package (with its own package.json).

```
mkdir -p packages/community-nodes/my-custom-node

cd packages/community-nodes/my-custom-node
```

2. Define package metadata

```
{

  "name": "n8n-nodes-my-custom-node",

  "version": "1.0.0",

  "description": "Custom node for n8n",

  "main": "dist/index.js",

  "author": "Your Name",

  "license": "MIT",

  "scripts": {
```

```
    "build": "tsc"
  }
}
```

3. Publish to npm

```
npm publish
```

4. Install the Node in Any n8n Instance

```
npm install n8n-nodes-my-custom-node
```

Then run:

```
n8n start --tunnel
```

Best Practices for Node Sharing

Practice	Description
Proper Naming	Use the n8n-nodes- prefix
Versioning	Follow semantic versioning (e.g., 1.0.0)
Clear Documentation	Include README.md with usage and parameters
License Specification	Choose an open-source license (e.g., MIT)
Follow n8n's Contribution Guide	Align with formatting and standards

Key Takeaways

- Community nodes extend n8n's ecosystem and encourage reuse.
- Packaging and publishing nodes as npm packages is straightforward.

- Documentation is crucial for adoption and reuse.

11.5 Publishing on npm and GitHub

Once you've developed a custom n8n node, you can share it with the world via **npm** and **GitHub**. This makes it easier for others to discover, install, and contribute to your node. This section walks through packaging, publishing, and best practices for distribution.

Learning Objectives

- Prepare and structure your custom node for publishing.
- Publish your package to **npm**.
- Share your code on **GitHub** with best practices.

A. Preparing the Node Package

Ensure the project structure is clean and complete:

n8n-nodes-my-node/

├── dist/

├── src/

├── package.json

├── README.md

├── LICENSE

└── tsconfig.json

B. Configuring package.json

Use semantic naming and versioning:

```
{

 "name": "n8n-nodes-my-node",

 "version": "1.0.0",

 "description": "An n8n node for interacting with XYZ API",

 "main": "dist/index.js",
```

```
"types": "dist/index.d.ts",

"scripts": {

  "build": "tsc",

  "prepare": "npm run build"

},

"keywords": ["n8n", "automation", "node"],

"author": "Your Name",

"license": "MIT",

"dependencies": {

  "n8n-workflow": "^1.0.0",

  "n8n-core": "^1.0.0"

}

}
```

C. Publishing to npm

Step-by-Step Guide

Login to npm:

```
npm login
```

1. **Build the project:**

```
npm run build
```

2. **Publish it:**

```
npm publish --access public
```

3. Once published, your node will be accessible from:

https://www.npmjs.com/package/n8n-nodes-my-node

D. Sharing on GitHub

Steps to Upload

1. Create a new repository at github.com/new

Initialize and push your local project:

```
git init

git add .

git commit -m "Initial commit"

git remote add origin https://github.com/your-username/n8n-nodes-my-node.git

git push -u origin master
```

2. Add topics (e.g., n8n, automation, custom-node) in the repo settings.

E. Flowchart: Node Publication Workflow

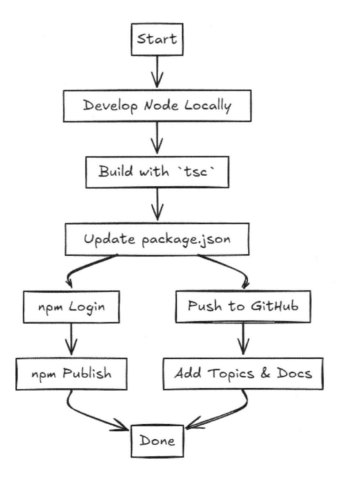

F. Best Practices

Area	Recommendation
Documentation	Include setup, parameters, and usage in the README.md
Versioning	Follow Semantic Versioning (1.0.0, 1.1.0, etc.)
GitHub Tags	Create releases using GitHub tags
License	Use open-source licenses (MIT, Apache 2.0, etc.)
Community Support	Enable Issues and Discussions for contributions and help

G. Sample README Table Format

Field	Description
Name	The name of your node package
Version	Current stable version
description	A short description of what your node does

Install	npm install n8n-nodes-my-node
Usage	Explain input/output fields, node configuration

Summary

- Publishing your node makes it reusable and accessible to the broader community.
- Use **npm** for distribution and **GitHub** for collaboration.
- Maintain clean structure, semantic versions, and helpful documentation.

Chapter 12: Deployment and Scaling

Chapter Objectives

- Understand deployment options: cloud, self-hosted, and hybrid
- Learn best practices for scaling workflows for large volumes
- Set up monitoring, logging, and performance optimization
- Ensure backup, versioning, and failover for reliability

12.1 Self-Hosting: Docker, VPS, Cloud

n8n can be hosted on various platforms, giving you flexibility and control over your automation environment. This section provides a step-by-step guide to deploying n8n on **Docker**, **VPS**, and **cloud providers**.

Learning Objectives

- Understand self-hosting options for n8n.
- Deploy n8n on Docker, VPS, and cloud platforms.
- Configure basic runtime settings and environment variables.

A. Hosting Options Overview (Table)

Method	Description	Pros	Cons
Docker	Containerized deployment on any OS	Easy setup, portable	Requires Docker knowledge
VPS	Manual setup on Linux servers	Full control, customizable	Requires system admin skills
Cloud (e.g., AWS, DigitalOcean)	Managed or semi-managed deployment	Scalable, on-demand pricing	Complex for beginners

B. Docker Deployment (Step-by-Step)

Pre-requisites:

- Docker installed
- Docker Compose (optional but recommended)

Basic Setup

```yaml
# docker-compose.yml

version: '3.1'

services:

 n8n:

  image: n8nio/n8n

  restart: always

  ports:

   - "5678:5678"

  environment:

   - N8N_BASIC_AUTH_ACTIVE=true

   - N8N_BASIC_AUTH_USER=admin

   - N8N_BASIC_AUTH_PASSWORD=yourpassword

   - DB_TYPE=sqlite

   - N8N_HOST=localhost
```

Commands to Run:

```
docker-compose up -d
```

C. VPS Deployment

Steps to Deploy on Ubuntu VPS

1. **Update & Install Node.js:**

```
sudo apt update && sudo apt install nodejs npm -y
```

2. **Install n8n Globally:**

```
npm install n8n -g
```

3. **Run n8n as Background Process (Optional with PM2):**

```
n8n
```

For persistent background service:

```
npm install pm2 -g

pm2 start n8n

pm2 save
```

D. Cloud Deployment Tips

Cloud Provider	Notes
AWS EC2	Use Ubuntu AMI, set up with security groups and SSL
DigitalOcean	One-click Docker droplets simplify the setup
Render/Heroku	Offers managed infrastructure with GitHub CI integration

E. Environment Configuration (Flowchart)

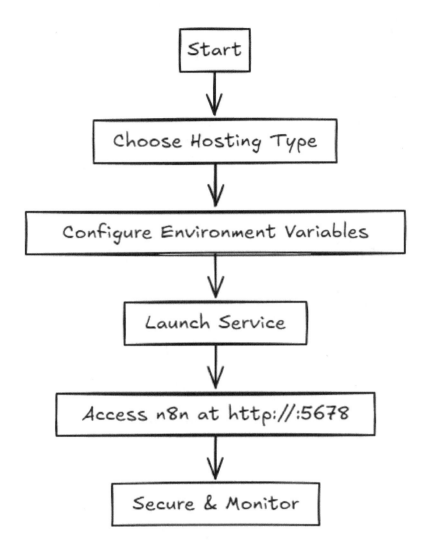

Key Takeaways

- Docker is ideal for quick local or server deployment.
- VPS allows full control but requires more configuration.
- Cloud hosting adds scalability but may involve extra setup.
- Always secure with authentication and HTTPS in production.

12.2 Scaling for High-Volume Automation

As workflows grow in complexity and traffic, scaling n8n becomes essential. This section covers **horizontal and vertical scaling strategies**, **job queue configurations**, and **best practices** for handling high-throughput automation workloads.

Learning Objectives

- Understand strategies for scaling n8n.
- Differentiate between horizontal and vertical scaling.
- Configure n8n for distributed execution using queues.
- Learn best practices for high-performance workflows.

A. Scaling Strategies (Table)

Strategy	Description	Use Case
Vertical Scaling	Increase CPU/RAM of the server	Single instance under heavy load
Horizontal Scaling	Run multiple instances behind a load balancer	High availability and concurrent jobs
Queue Mode	Use Redis to manage job distribution	Asynchronous execution for scalability

B. Horizontal Scaling with Queue Mode

n8n supports **queue mode**, enabling you to **distribute execution** across multiple workers.

Components Required:

- Redis (for queue management)
- Multiple worker instances
- Load balancer (e.g., NGINX)

Environment Variables (for Queue Mode)

```
EXECUTIONS_MODE=queue

QUEUE_MODE_REDIS_HOST=redis

QUEUE_MODE_REDIS_PORT=6379

N8N_WORKFLOW_EXECUTIONS_MODE=queue
```

Flowchart: Queue-Based Scaling

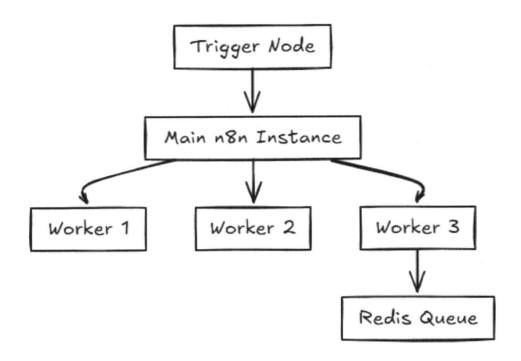

C. Load Balancer Configuration (Basic)

Use **NGINX** or **HAProxy** to route traffic across multiple n8n frontends.

```
upstream n8n {

   server 127.0.0.1:5678;

   server 127.0.0.1:5679;

}


server {
```

```
listen 80;

location / {

    proxy_pass http://n8n;

}

}
```

D. Workflow Optimization Tips

Tip	Benefit
Use Sub-Workflows	Reduce load on main workflows
Minimize use of heavy Function nodes	Improve execution speed
Avoid excessive polling	Lower resource consumption
Use caching where possible	Reduce redundant API calls

Key Takeaways

- Queue mode enables high-performance, distributed execution.
- Use Redis, load balancers, and multiple instances for scalability.
- Design workflows with efficiency in mind to reduce strain on infrastructure.

12.3 Performance Monitoring & Metrics

Monitoring your n8n instance is crucial to ensure **system health**, detect **bottlenecks**, and **maintain uptime**. In this section, we explore tools and techniques to track metrics, log performance, and visualize execution health.

Learning Objectives

- Track performance and error logs.

- Use tools like Prometheus and Grafana.
- Monitor execution times and resource usage.

A. Monitoring Options (Table)

Tool	Purpose	Integration Example
Prometheus	Metric collection	Use node_exporter + n8n stats
Grafana	Visualize Prometheus data	Create dashboards with key metrics
Logrotate	Manage log files on VPS	Rotate logs to avoid overflow
PM2 Dashboard	Monitor Node.js process health	Shows memory, CPU, restarts

B. Useful Metrics to Monitor

- **Active Executions**
- **Failed Jobs Count**
- **Execution Time (avg, max)**
- **CPU & RAM Usage**
- **Worker Queue Size**

C. Prometheus + Grafana Flowchart

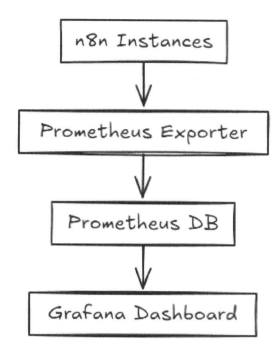

D. Tips for Stable Monitoring

- Set alerts for failed executions or high CPU load.
- Use persistent logging for debugging.
- Keep dashboard filters for time window and execution types.

Key Takeaways

- Regular monitoring ensures reliable automation at scale.
- Tools like Prometheus and Grafana provide actionable insights.
- Set thresholds and alerts to detect problems early.

12.4 Logging and Alerting

Logging and alerting are essential for maintaining automation stability, identifying failures, and ensuring visibility into workflow execution. This section covers how to configure logging and implement alerting mechanisms in both self-hosted and cloud environments.

Learning Objectives

- Understand types of logs n8n provides.

- Configure persistent logging (file, syslog, external services).
- Set up alerting for failed or slow executions.

A. Types of Logs in n8n

Log Type	Description	Example
Execution Logs	Detailed logs of each workflow execution	Success/failure, input/output
System Logs	Server-level info (startup, shutdown, errors)	Port listening, worker started
Console Logs	General logs printed to stdout/stderr	console.log() in Function Node

B. Enabling Logging (Self-Hosted)

Environment Variables

```
N8N_LOG_LEVEL=info

N8N_LOG_OUTPUT=file

N8N_LOG_FILE_LOCATION=/home/n8n/logs/n8n.log

Log levels: error, warn, info, verbose, debug
```

Best Practices

- Rotate logs using **logrotate**.
- Use **external log management** (e.g., ELK stack, Papertrail, Datadog).

C. Alerting Mechanisms

Method	Description
Email Alerts	Send emails on execution failure
Slack/Discord Alerts	Webhook notifications for team visibility
Monitoring Tools	Use Grafana alerts based on Prometheus data

Example: Email on Failure (Simplified Workflow)

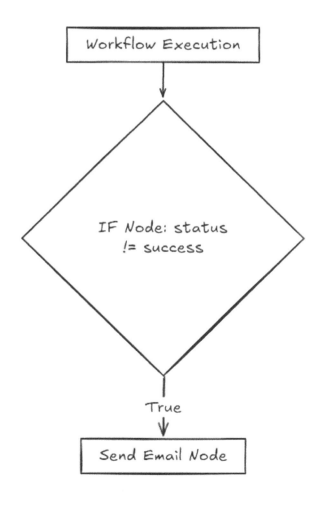

D. Alerting Best Practices

- **Filter noise:** Only alert on critical workflows.
- **Set thresholds:** Alert if execution time > X or failure count > Y.
- **Centralize alerts:** Route to a single dashboard or channel.

Key Takeaways

- Enable and manage persistent logs for audit and debugging.
- Set up alerts for failures and anomalies.
- Combine logs and alerts for proactive automation maintenance.

12.5 Workflow Versioning and Backups

As workflows evolve, **version control** and **backups** become vital. This section covers how to manage versions of your workflows, back up your n8n data, and use Git-based practices to track changes.

Learning Objectives

- Version and backup workflows safely.
- Use CLI or API for exporting/importing workflows.
- Integrate Git for audit and rollback.

A. Workflow Export & Import

CLI Command

```
n8n export:workflow --id=<workflow_id> --output=workflow.json

n8n import:workflow --input=workflow.json
```

API Approach

- Use /rest/workflows endpoint to fetch and store JSON workflows.
- Automate export on save using n8n webhooks.

B. Workflow Versioning with Git

Step	Tool/Method
Export workflows daily	Cron + CLI
Commit to Git repo	Git CLI or GitHub API
Track diffs and changes	Git log + Git diff
Rollback to old version	Git revert + import

C. Backup Strategies

Component	Backup Frequency	Tool
Workflows (JSON)	Daily	n8n export + Git
Environment (.env)	Weekly	Encrypted vault or GPG
Database (SQLite/DB)	Daily	pg_dump, mongodump, etc.

D. Flowchart: Backup & Version Control

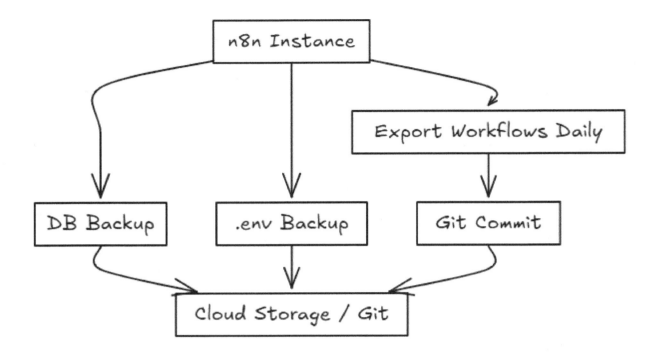

Key Takeaways

- Automate workflow exports and back them up regularly.
- Use Git for version control, auditing, and rollback.
- Protect environment files and DB snapshots securely.

Chapter 13: Real-World Projects & Case Studies

Chapter Objectives

- Apply n8n workflows to solve real-world business problems
- Understand architecture, logic, and challenges of practical automation projects
- Explore case studies across industries like e-commerce, healthcare, finance, and marketing

---

13.1 Social Media Scheduling System

Objective

Build a workflow that automates social media post scheduling across multiple platforms like X (Twitter), LinkedIn, and Facebook using n8n.

Use Case

A digital marketer wants to queue posts and have them published at set times without manual intervention.

Workflow Overview

1. **Trigger:** Cron Node (runs hourly or daily)
2. **Data Source:** Google Sheets or Airtable (post queue)
3. **Filter:** Posts scheduled for the current time
4. **Logic:** Format content per platform
5. **Action:** Post using X, LinkedIn, Facebook nodes
6. **Log:** Record success/failure in a database or sheet

Flowchart

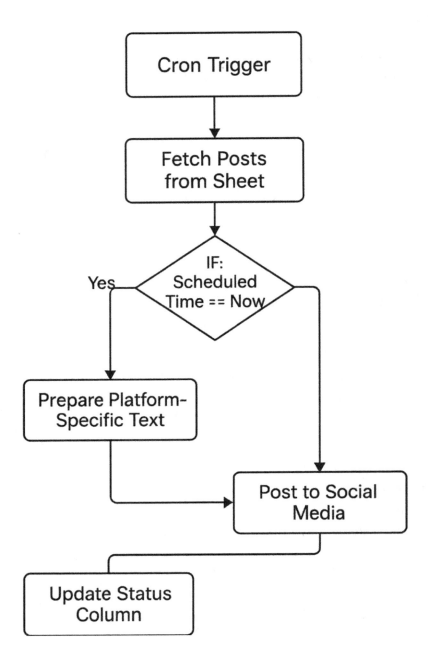

Tips

- Use environment variables for API tokens.
- Delay posting to avoid rate limits.
- Track logs for auditing via a Notion or Airtable DB.

13.2 Lead Capture & CRM Integration

Objective

Automate capturing leads from a web form and adding them to a CRM like HubSpot, Salesforce, or Pipedrive.

Use Case

A company collects leads via a website contact form and wants them instantly recorded in their CRM and notified via email or Slack.

Workflow Overview

1. **Trigger:** Webhook Node connected to form
2. **Validation:** Ensure fields (name, email) are valid
3. **Check:** Duplicate check in CRM
4. **Action:** Create or update contact in CRM
5. **Notification:** Send confirmation email and Slack alert

Flowchart

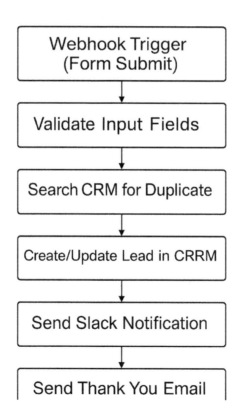

Enhancements

- Enrich leads using a tool like Clearbit.
- Tag leads based on UTM parameters.
- Store backup in Google Sheets for redundancy.

13.3 Customer Feedback Classifier with AI

Objective

Automatically classify customer feedback by sentiment (positive, neutral, negative) and topic (e.g., pricing, support, features) using AI services like OpenAI or Claude, and route insights for action.

Use Case

A SaaS business receives customer reviews and feedback via forms, email, or chat. They want to process the feedback in real-time, label it, and send it to the appropriate team.

Workflow Overview

1. **Trigger:** Webhook (feedback form) or Email node
2. **AI Classification:** Use OpenAI API for sentiment + topic classification
3. **Routing:** Route to different teams based on topic
4. **Logging:** Save to a feedback database or Google Sheet
5. **Notification:** Send summary to Slack or email

Flowchart

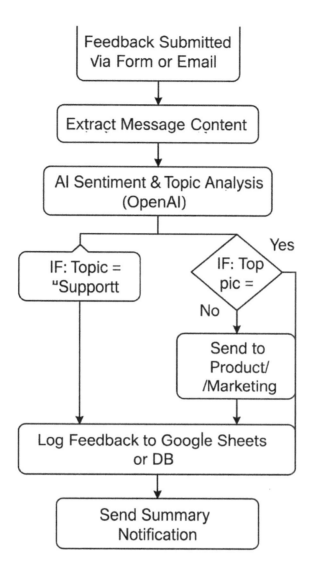

Enhancements

- Highlight negative feedback for escalation.
- Create tags or scores for prioritization.
- Weekly digest of categorized feedback.

13.4 Support Ticket Auto-Routing

Objective

Automatically route incoming support tickets to the right team or agent based on keyword analysis, priority, and availability.

Use Case

A customer support team receives tickets via email, form, or CRM. They want to reduce manual triage time by automating categorization and routing.

Workflow Overview

1. **Trigger:** Email or Webhook (ticket submission)
2. **Text Parsing:** Extract key fields from ticket
3. **Priority Check:** Detect urgency via subject/body
4. **Category Matching:** Use keyword or AI classification
5. **Routing:** Assign to support agent/team
6. **Logging:** Update ticketing system (e.g., Zendesk, Freshdesk)
7. **Notify:** Send assignment alert to agent

Flowchart

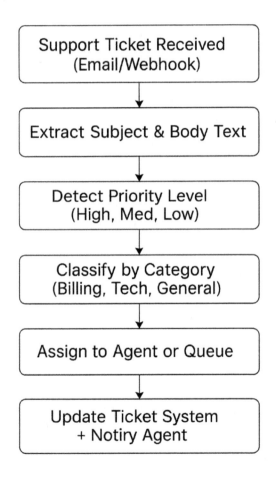

Enhancements

- Escalate high-priority tickets after timeout.
- Use AI to analyze sentiment or urgency.
- Sync with CRM for customer context before routing.

13.5 Auto-Sync Blog Posts Across Platforms

Objective

Automatically synchronize published blog content across multiple platforms such as Medium, WordPress, LinkedIn, and Dev.to whenever a new post is published.

Use Case

A content team manages a central blog and wants to distribute the same content to other platforms for reach and consistency, without manual reposting.

Workflow Overview

1. **Trigger:** New blog post detected (RSS Feed or CMS Webhook)
2. **Content Fetch:** Retrieve full post content via HTTP or API
3. **Format Conversion:** Adjust formatting for each platform (Markdown, HTML)
4. **Cross-Post:** Publish to Medium, WordPress, LinkedIn, Dev.to via respective APIs
5. **Log & Notify:** Log published URLs and send confirmation

Flowchart

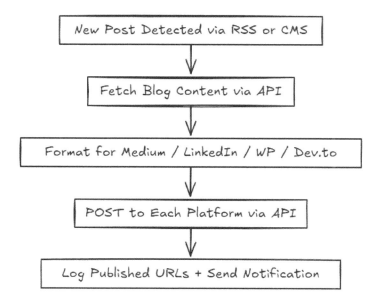

Enhancements

- Auto-schedule posts at optimal times.
- Use tags and categories dynamically.
- Track click performance using UTM codes.

13.6 Automated Invoice & Payment Notifications

Objective

Generate invoices and send automated payment reminders based on billing cycle and payment status from a database or financial system.

Use Case

A freelancer or SaaS business needs to automate invoice creation, delivery, and payment follow-ups for better cash flow and reduced admin tasks.

Workflow Overview

1. **Trigger:** Scheduled (Cron) or new payment entry
2. **Invoice Generator:** Use Function or PDF generator to create invoice
3. **Send Invoice:** Email invoice via SMTP or transactional email service
4. **Monitor Payments:** Poll payment provider (e.g., Stripe, PayPal)
5. **Reminder:** If unpaid after X days, send a follow-up email
6. **Logging:** Record sent status in Google Sheets, DB, or Airtable

Flowchart

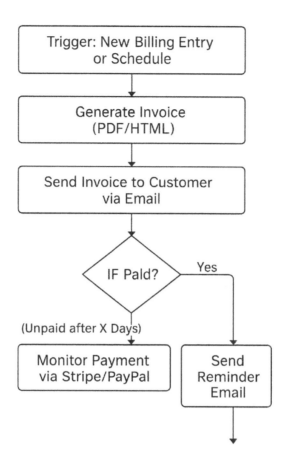

Enhancements

- Add payment links directly in emails.
- Auto-generate late fee notices after a grace period.
- Sync with accounting tools like QuickBooks or Xero.

13.7 Industry-Specific Case Studies

This section presents practical automation use cases tailored to specific industries, demonstrating how n8n can solve real-world problems through streamlined workflows.

13.7.1 Healthcare: Automating Patient Data Handling

Objective:

Streamline the collection, processing, and distribution of patient data using n8n to reduce manual input, improve accuracy, and ensure timely access to medical information.

Learning Outcomes:

By the end of this section, readers will be able to:

- Integrate healthcare form submissions or EHR/EMR APIs with n8n.
- Automate the storage, tagging, and distribution of patient data.
- Implement privacy-aware workflows aligned with data protection standards (e.g., HIPAA/GDPR).
- Notify staff in real-time when critical patient data is received.

Use Case Scenario:

A clinic uses a digital form to collect patient intake details. The data needs to be automatically stored in a secure system, tagged for urgency, and emailed to assigned practitioners.

Flowchart:

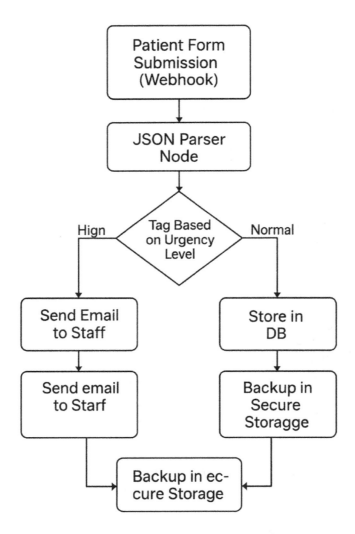

Step-by-Step Workflow Implementation:

1. **Webhook Trigger:**
   - Connect to form platforms like **Typeform**, **JotForm**, or a custom front-end using a **Webhook** node.
2. **JSON Parse / Set Node:**
   - Clean and structure the incoming data.
   - Ensure key fields (name, symptoms, urgency level) are standardized.
3. **Function Node:**
   - Tag records with priority levels based on keywords or symptom severity.

Example:

```
const urgency = item.json.symptoms.includes("chest pain") ? "high" : "normal";

item.json.urgency = urgency;

return [item];
```

4. **Switch Node:**
   - Route high-priority cases for immediate action (e.g., send to staff via email).
5. **Email Node:**
   - Notify doctors or nurses with patient details if flagged as urgent.
6. **Database / Airtable / Google Sheets Node:**
   - Log the full patient data for records and future access.
7. **File Node / FTP / Cloud Storage:**
   - Securely back up submitted forms or attachments in encrypted cloud storage.

Example Patient Intake Table:

Field	Example Value	Description
Name	Jane Doe	Patient full name
Symptoms	Chest pain, nausea	Used to assess urgency

Urgency Level	High	Calculated based on symptoms
Assigned To	Dr. A. Smith	Determined by routing rules
Timestamp	2025-05-02 09:32 AM	Time of form submission

Key Takeaways:

- Automate the flow of **clinical intake data** to reduce administrative overhead.
- Use **trigger-based logic** to prioritize urgent medical cases.
- Combine **conditional logic**, **email**, and **storage** nodes for complete workflow handling.
- Ensure **data backups and compliance** by integrating with secure cloud systems.

13.7.2 Finance: Automating Transaction Notifications

Objective:

Enable real-time financial alerts by monitoring transaction data from payment processors or bank APIs, ensuring instant visibility into income, expenses, or anomalies.

Learning Outcomes:

By the end of this section, the reader will be able to:

- Connect n8n to financial APIs or data sources.
- Filter and analyze transaction data.
- Send customized alerts based on amount, type, or metadata.
- Log transaction records into databases or Google Sheets.

Workflow Use Case:

A company wants to receive an instant alert every time a transaction exceeds $1,000 or matches specific keywords (e.g., "refund", "chargeback").

Flowchart:

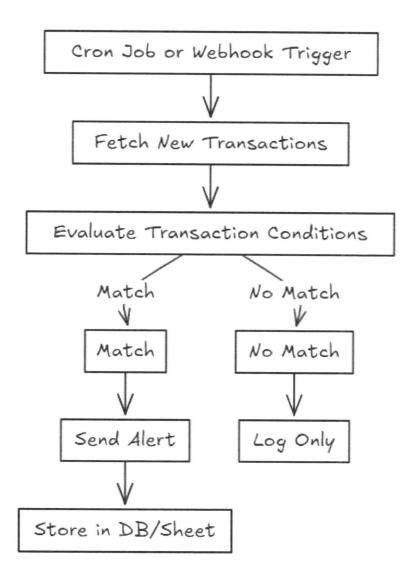

Step-by-Step Workflow Implementation:

1. **Trigger Node:**
   - Use a **Cron** node (e.g., every 10 minutes) or a **Webhook** from Stripe, PayPal, or your bank API.
2. **HTTP Request Node:**
   - Pull recent transaction data via API call.
   - Example: Stripe's /v1/charges endpoint.
3. **Function Node:**
   - Filter transactions exceeding a set threshold or containing keywords.

Example JavaScript:

```
return items.filter(item => {

  const amount = item.json.amount;

  const description = item.json.description.toLowerCase();

  return amount > 100000 || description.includes("refund") || description.includes("chargeback");

});
```

4. **If Node (Optional):**
   ○ Route high-value or suspicious transactions to a different alert mechanism.
5. **Email or Slack Node:**
   ○ Send a notification with relevant transaction details:
     ■ Amount
     ■ Description
     ■ Date
     ■ Customer Name
6. **Google Sheets / DB Node:**
   ○ Append the transaction to a spreadsheet or a PostgreSQL/MongoDB table for audit purposes.

Example Transaction Filter Table:

Field	Condition	Action
Amount	> $1,000	Send Email Alert
Description	Contains "refund"	Tag as Refund
Description	Contains "chargeback"	Escalate via Slack
Amount	< $50	No Alert (Log Only)

Key Takeaways:

- Use **cron** or **webhooks** to monitor financial transactions.
- Combine **Function Nodes** and **If Nodes** to create intelligent filters.
- Integrate **alerts** via email, chat, or SMS.
- Store or archive transaction data for future analysis or compliance.

13.7.3 E-Commerce: Inventory Sync and Order Fulfillment

Objective:

Automate inventory management and order processing across multiple sales channels using n8n, ensuring real-time sync and efficient fulfillment with minimal manual intervention.

Learning Outcomes:

By the end of this section, readers will be able to:

- Sync inventory between platforms like Shopify, WooCommerce, and Amazon.
- Automate order notifications and fulfillment actions.
- Integrate with shipping APIs and warehouse systems.
- Handle out-of-stock alerts and inventory thresholds with logic nodes.

Use Case Scenario:

An online retailer sells products on Shopify and Amazon. When a sale occurs on either platform, the inventory should update everywhere. Orders should be automatically forwarded to the fulfillment center, and customers should be notified with tracking info.

Flowchart:

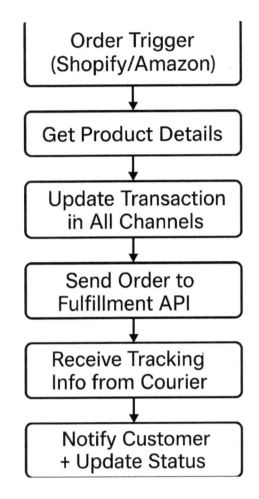

Step-by-Step Workflow Implementation:

1. **Trigger Node:**
   - Use **Shopify Trigger**, **Amazon Polling**, or **Webhook** for third-party order sources.
2. **HTTP Request / API Node:**
   - Fetch order details including product SKU, quantity, customer info.
3. **Set / Function Node:**
   - Extract and transform data for inventory updates.
4. **Multiple API Calls:**
   - Update inventory in all other platforms (e.g., WooCommerce, eBay) using REST API nodes.
5. **Conditional Logic (Switch/IF):**
   - If item stock falls below threshold, send notification to inventory manager or pause listings.

6. **Fulfillment Request (HTTP Request):**
   ○ Forward order to warehouse or fulfillment partner using their API.
7. **Polling for Tracking (Interval + HTTP):**
   ○ Periodically check for tracking status and update once available.
8. **Email / SMS Node:**
   ○ Notify customer with shipping confirmation and tracking number.

Example Inventory Sync Table:

Product SKU	Shopify Stock	Amazon Stock	Last Synced
ABC-123	12	10	2025-05-02 14:10 PM
XYZ-789	4	4	2025-05-02 14:10 PM

Example Fulfillment API Payload:

```
{

"order_id": "ORD123456",

"sku": "ABC-123",

"quantity": 2,

"customer": {

"name": "John Smith",

"address": "123 Main St, NY, USA"

}

}
```

Key Takeaways:

● Automate **real-time inventory synchronization** across multiple channels to avoid overselling.
● Forward orders to **fulfillment partners or internal warehouses** without manual steps.
● Use **conditional logic** to prevent stockouts and manage reorder workflows.

- Improve customer experience with **automated shipping updates** and **reliable order status tracking**.

13.7.4 Marketing: Campaign Automation and Reporting

Objective:

Use n8n to automate end-to-end marketing workflows—from launching multi-channel campaigns to tracking KPIs and generating reports for continuous improvement.

Learning Outcomes:

By the end of this section, readers will be able to:

- Automate email, social media, and ad campaign workflows.
- Integrate with marketing tools like Mailchimp, Meta Ads, and Google Analytics.
- Aggregate and visualize campaign performance data.
- Set up automated reports and KPI alerts.

Use Case Scenario:

A digital marketing team wants to launch a product campaign via email, Facebook Ads, and Twitter. They need automated tracking of click-through rates (CTR), conversions, and must receive daily reports on campaign health.

Flowchart:

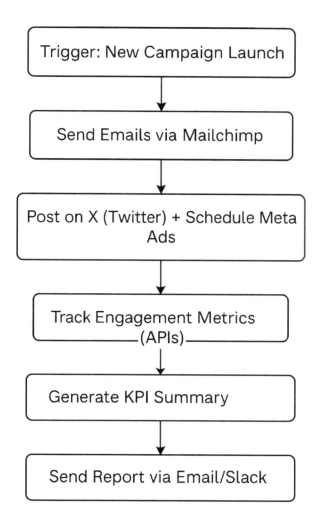

Step-by-Step Workflow Implementation:

1. **Trigger Node:**
   - Trigger manually or via a CMS/API when a campaign is ready.
2. **Email Automation:**
   - Use **Mailchimp Node** or **SMTP Node** to send campaign emails.
3. **Social Media Posting:**
   - Connect **X (Twitter), Facebook Ads, Instagram**, or **LinkedIn API** via **HTTP Request** or **official n8n nodes**.
4. **Tracking Metrics:**
   - Use **Google Analytics**, **Meta Ads Insights**, or **UTM Tracking** with API calls to pull performance metrics.
5. **Set / Function Node:**

- Process and aggregate the fetched metrics into meaningful KPIs (e.g., CTR, bounce rate, conversion rate).

6. **Daily Scheduler:**
   - Use **Cron Node** to schedule daily or weekly reporting workflows.

7. **Email or Slack Report:**
   - Format campaign performance summary and send it via **Email Node** or **Slack Node**.

Example KPI Table:

Metric	Value	Goal	Status
Email Open Rate	43%	>35%	Pass
CTR (Ads + Email)	5.6%	>4%	Pass
Conversions	38	>50	Under
Bounce Rate	28%	<30%	Pass

Example Email Report Snippet:

Subject: Campaign Report – Week of May 1

Hi Team,

Here's the latest performance snapshot:

- Email Open Rate: 43%

- CTR: 5.6%

- Total Conversions: 38

- Bounce Rate: 28%

Recommendations:

- A/B test subject lines for better conversions.

- Increase ad spend for high-performing creatives.

Regards,

Marketing Automation Bot

Key Takeaways:

- Use n8n to automate **cross-channel marketing actions** from a single workflow.
- Integrate with major platforms for **data aggregation and analytics**.
- Set up **daily or weekly KPI reports** to stay informed and optimize campaigns.
- Reduce manual reporting and gain real-time visibility into campaign effectiveness.

Chapter 14: Monetize Your n8n Skills

Objective:

In this chapter, we'll explore how to turn your expertise in n8n into a source of income. Whether you're a freelancer, consultant, or aspiring product creator, this chapter will guide you through the steps to monetize your n8n skills.

Learning Outcomes:

By the end of this chapter, readers will:

- Understand the different ways to monetize their n8n expertise.
- Learn how to package and sell workflow templates.
- Explore opportunities for freelancing, consulting, and teaching.
- Gain insights into building a personal brand and finding clients.

14.1 Freelancing and Consulting

Freelancing and consulting offer flexible and lucrative ways to monetize your n8n skills. By helping clients streamline their operations, improve efficiency, and automate routine tasks, you can create a sustainable income stream while gaining real-world experience. Here's how you can start freelancing and consulting with n8n:

1. Define Your Services

The first step in starting as a freelancer or consultant is clearly defining the services you will offer. This allows you to focus on a niche and tailor your skills to meet specific client needs.

Key Services to Offer:

- **Custom Workflow Design:**
  - Build custom automation solutions for businesses, including marketing workflows, customer support automation, and CRM integrations.
- **Consultation and Strategy:**
  - Help clients assess their needs and create a roadmap for automating business processes using n8n. Provide advice on how automation can save time and increase productivity.
- **API Integration:**

- Integrate third-party APIs with n8n to streamline processes like syncing data between SaaS applications (e.g., integrating CRM tools with email platforms, or linking project management systems).
- **Automated Reporting and Notifications:**
  - Set up systems that automatically generate reports or send notifications based on triggers like sales, inventory levels, or customer interactions.
- **System Optimization and Maintenance:**
  - Help businesses maintain and optimize existing workflows, ensuring they run efficiently and are updated to take advantage of new features or services.

Focus Areas:

- **Marketing Automation:** Lead nurturing, email campaigns, social media scheduling.
- **E-commerce Automation:** Inventory management, order fulfillment, and customer communication.
- **CRM Integration:** Synchronizing customer data between various platforms.
- **Custom Data Workflows:** Automating data handling, reporting, and analysis.

By identifying a few core services that align with your expertise and market demand, you can start by offering specialized packages.

2. Find Clients

Once you've defined your services, the next step is to find clients who need your expertise. There are various avenues you can explore to find your first freelancing or consulting gig.

Where to Find Clients:

- **Freelance Platforms:**
  - **Upwork:** Offers a wide range of automation-related jobs. You can create a profile that highlights your n8n expertise, bid on relevant projects, and get started quickly.
  - **Fiverr:** A platform for smaller gigs, where you can create service packages like "I will automate your email marketing with n8n" or "Create a custom CRM automation system."
  - **Freelancer:** Similar to Upwork, but often with shorter-term projects.
- **Social Media and Professional Networks:**
  - **LinkedIn:** Share case studies, articles, and success stories about n8n automation to attract attention. Reach out directly to business owners and managers who could benefit from automation.
  - **Twitter:** Join discussions around automation, SaaS tools, and no-code platforms. Share tips, tutorials, and your services.

- o **Facebook Groups:** Join business automation or specific industry-related groups where you can offer your services.
- **Networking and Referrals:**
  - o Start by offering your services to friends, family, and colleagues. Ask for referrals once you complete successful projects.
  - o Attend local or online tech meetups, workshops, or conferences related to automation or your niche (e.g., e-commerce, marketing, etc.).
- **Direct Outreach:**
  - o Identify businesses that could benefit from automation and contact them directly. For example, if you notice a local business relies on manual tasks that could be automated, propose a solution.

3. Create a Portfolio

A portfolio is essential for demonstrating your capabilities and gaining the trust of potential clients. It allows you to showcase your previous work and highlight your expertise.

Building a Portfolio:

- **Showcase Your Work:**
  - o Share workflows you've built, focusing on the problem it solved and the benefits it brought to the client (e.g., "This workflow saved the client 10 hours a week by automating manual data entry").
- **Create Case Studies:**
  - o Write detailed case studies for the workflows you've built. Discuss the business problem, your approach, and the results (e.g., increased sales conversion, streamlined communication, reduced costs).
- **Client Testimonials:**
  - o After completing a project, ask satisfied clients for testimonials that can be shared on your website or profiles. Positive feedback builds credibility.
- **Public Portfolio:**
  - o Consider using **GitHub** or your own website to share reusable workflow templates, code snippets, or even complete projects (with client consent). This shows potential clients that you can deliver practical and results-driven solutions.

4. Pricing Your Services

Setting the right price for your services is crucial to attracting clients while also making sure you're compensated fairly. There are various pricing models you can choose from.

Pricing Models:

- **Hourly Rate:**
  - Great for smaller, short-term projects. Charge based on the complexity and duration of the work required. Hourly rates can vary depending on your experience, location, and market demand.
  - Example: $50–$150 per hour, depending on experience and complexity.
- **Project-Based Pricing:**
  - Charge a flat fee for the completion of a specific project. For example, "I will automate your lead generation process for $500."
  - This model is suitable for well-defined projects with clear deliverables.
- **Retainer Model:**
  - Offer ongoing services, such as maintaining and optimizing automated workflows over time. This is ideal for long-term relationships with clients.
  - Example: $1,000 per month for continued support and workflow optimization.
- **Consultation Fee:**
  - Charge for one-time consultations or audits where you analyze a company's current processes and suggest ways to automate and improve efficiency.
  - Example: $200 per consultation or hourly for strategy sessions.

5. Contract and Communication Best Practices

Once you've attracted clients, it's essential to have clear communication and solid agreements in place.

Key Best Practices:

- **Set Clear Expectations:**
  - Ensure that both parties agree on the scope of work, timelines, deliverables, and pricing. Be clear about what is included in the service and what constitutes additional work (e.g., further revisions, additional workflows).
- **Use Contracts:**
  - Always work with a written contract to protect both you and your clients. Contracts should outline the project details, timelines, payment terms, and intellectual property rights.
- **Communication:**
  - Maintain open communication throughout the project. Use tools like **Trello, Slack,** or **Asana** to keep clients updated on progress.
  - Be proactive in addressing concerns and questions and ensure the client knows exactly when and how you will deliver the project.

14.2 Building and Selling Workflow Templates

Objective:

Learn how to design, package, and monetize reusable workflow templates for businesses and individual users using n8n.

Learning Outcomes:

By the end of this section, readers will:

- Understand how to design reusable and adaptable workflow templates.
- Learn packaging and documentation best practices.
- Discover platforms and strategies to sell or license templates.
- Know how to price, promote, and support workflow products.

What Are Workflow Templates?

Workflow templates in n8n are prebuilt automation blueprints that solve a specific task—such as "Lead to CRM Sync" or "New Blog Post to Social Media Distribution." These templates save time and are valuable to individuals or teams with recurring automation needs.

Template Creation Workflow:

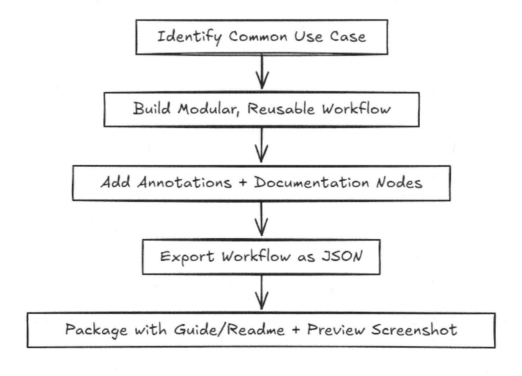

Tips for Building Sellable Templates:

- **Keep it Generic:** Use placeholder credentials and variables so it's easy for others to adapt.
- **Add Documentation:** Include usage instructions and required integrations.
- **Optimize for Simplicity:** Use sub-workflows and Set nodes to keep it readable.
- **Test Thoroughly:** Ensure it handles edge cases and error scenarios.

Where to Sell Your Templates:

Platform	Monetization Method	Notes
Gumroad	Direct sales	Easy setup, good for digital goods.
Etsy	Digital download	For non-tech buyers, simple storefront
Fiverr/Upwork	Custom setup gigs	Build income via service + template
Own Website	License or subscription	Total control, brand authority
n8n Community Forum	Free samples + upselling	Great for exposure and niche presence

Pricing Models:

- **One-Time Purchase:** Ideal for niche solutions.
- **Subscription Access:** Bundle multiple templates and provide regular updates.
- **Freemium:** Offer free basic version with a paid advanced edition.
- **Custom License:** Offer tailored rights for agency or enterprise usage.

Example Template Ideas:

Template Name	Use Case	Potential Buyers
Social Media Syndication Bot	Cross-post blogs to X, LinkedIn, FB	Content creators, marketers
Lead Auto-Nurture Sequence	Email follow-up based on form leads	Agencies, startups, consultants
Automated Daily Standup Reporter	Summarize team Slack updates to email	Remote teams, managers
Shopify Order to Airtable Sync	Sales database tracking	E-commerce store owners
New GitHub Issue Notification Bot	Developer alert system via Slack	Dev teams, project managers

Packaging Checklist:

- JSON export of workflow
- README with setup instructions
- Annotated screenshots
- Video or GIF demo (optional)
- Terms of use/license
- Support contact or FAQ

Key Takeaways:

- Workflow templates are a scalable digital product with passive income potential.
- Focus on solving real-world problems with clear, simple, and well-documented solutions.
- Choose a monetization strategy aligned with your target audience and brand.
- Build authority by sharing knowledge, offering support, and gathering testimonials.

14.3 Creating Courses or YouTube Tutorials

Creating courses or YouTube tutorials is another excellent way to monetize your n8n skills. Sharing your knowledge with others not only establishes you as an expert but can also generate a passive income stream. Here's how you can get started:

1. Choose Your Platform

There are several platforms where you can sell your courses or post tutorials. The choice of platform depends on your audience and content format.

- **Udemy / Skillshare / Teachable:**
  These are popular platforms where you can create and sell full courses. These platforms offer a large audience, marketing support, and built-in tools to track learner progress.
- **YouTube:**
  YouTube is ideal for free tutorials, building an audience, and monetizing through ads and sponsorships. It's a great way to reach a broader audience while establishing a community.
- **Patreon:**
  If you prefer a subscription-based model, Patreon can be a good platform. You can offer exclusive tutorials, resources, and one-on-one coaching to patrons who pay a monthly fee.
- **Personal Website:**
  Hosting your courses on your website gives you full control over pricing, marketing, and customer interaction. It also allows you to capture leads and integrate marketing automation.

2. Define Your Course Topics

Start by identifying key topics within n8n that your target audience will find valuable. You can design beginner, intermediate, and advanced-level courses to cater to various skill levels.

Course Ideas:

- **to n8n:**
  - A beginner course covering installation, setting up workflows, and basic automation concepts.
- **Mastering n8n Workflows:**
  - In-depth exploration of complex workflows, conditional logic, API integrations, and advanced data manipulation.
- **n8n for Specific Use Cases:**

- Courses tailored to specific industries or tools (e.g., automating marketing processes with n8n, creating workflows for e-commerce automation).
- **Advanced n8n Development:**
  - Focus on custom nodes, creating reusable templates, and integrating with external services using advanced coding techniques.
- **Automating Business Processes with n8n:**
  - A practical course for entrepreneurs and business owners, focusing on automating common business processes like CRM integrations, customer support, and social media management.

3. Plan Your Content

Once you've decided on your course topics, create a detailed course outline. Organize your content logically, ensuring that it builds progressively. Some things to consider include:

- **Course Structure:**
  - Break your course into modules and lessons. Each lesson should cover a specific topic and include examples, code snippets, and practical demonstrations.
- **Hands-On Projects:**
  - Provide practical assignments or challenges at the end of each module. This encourages active learning and engagement.
- **Quizzes and Assessments:**
  - Use quizzes and assessments to test learners' understanding. This also adds value to your courses and can increase the perceived quality of your offerings.
- **Clear and Concise Explanation:**
  - Keep explanations simple, especially for beginners. Use a mix of visuals (e.g., diagrams, flowcharts) and real-world examples to make complex concepts easier to understand.

4. Record and Edit Your Content

Creating high-quality, engaging video content is crucial for maintaining learner interest. Here's how to approach this:

- **Equipment and Software:**
  - Invest in a good microphone and screen recording software (e.g., OBS Studio, Camtasia, or ScreenFlow) to ensure your audio and video are clear. For editing, use software like Adobe Premiere Pro or Final Cut Pro.
- **Engaging Presentation:**
  - Speak clearly and pace your tutorials so that learners can follow along easily. Add text overlays and annotations for clarity. Keep your videos concise and engaging.
- **Interactive Elements:**

- Include questions or prompts for learners to think about as they watch. Encourage them to pause the video and try out the concepts themselves.

5. Market and Sell Your Courses

Once your course is ready, it's time to market it. Utilize a variety of marketing techniques to drive traffic and gain sales or views:

- **Social Media Marketing:**
  - Share snippets of your content on platforms like LinkedIn, Twitter, and Instagram to attract learners. Post behind-the-scenes looks at your course creation process to build anticipation.
- **Email Marketing:**
  - Build an email list and send targeted newsletters or offers related to your course. This helps you reach an audience that's already interested in your content.
- **Free Content to Attract Followers:**
  - Create free content (e.g., short tutorials on YouTube or free course lessons) to build trust and encourage people to pay for the full course.
- **Collaborations and Partnerships:**
  - Partner with other educators or influencers in the automation or tech space to cross-promote each other's work.
- **Offer Discounts and Promotions:**
  - When launching your course, offer limited-time discounts or bonuses for early sign-ups. This can encourage more people to enroll.

6. Monetizing Your YouTube Channel

If you prefer YouTube, you can monetize your channel through ads, sponsorships, and affiliate marketing.

- **Ad Revenue:**
  - Once you meet the criteria (1,000 subscribers and 4,000 watch hours), you can enable ads on your videos. This is a passive income stream that generates money as people watch your content.
- **Affiliate Marketing:**
  - Promote tools and platforms related to automation (like Zapier, n8n, or hosting services) and earn a commission for each sale made through your affiliate links.
- **Sponsorships:**
  - Once your channel grows, you can attract sponsors who want to promote their products or services in your videos. This can provide a steady income stream.

14.4 Building SaaS or Microservices with n8n

Building a Software-as-a-Service (SaaS) or microservice using n8n is a powerful way to monetize your automation skills by providing solutions that help businesses or individuals automate tasks without needing to develop complex infrastructure.

1. Identify a Niche or Problem

To build a successful SaaS or microservice, start by identifying a specific problem that businesses or users face. This problem should be one that can be automated and solved using n8n workflows.

Example Ideas:

- **Automated Social Media Management Service:**
  A tool that automates the posting of social media content across platforms, manages content calendars, and tracks engagement.
- **CRM and Lead Management Automation:**
  A SaaS product that integrates with CRMs (like Salesforce, HubSpot) and automates lead capturing, follow-ups, and reporting.
- **Task and Project Automation for Teams:**
  Build a tool that automates task assignment, progress tracking, and team collaboration by integrating with project management tools (e.g., Asana, Trello, or Jira).
- **E-commerce Order Fulfillment Automation:**
  A SaaS tool that integrates e-commerce platforms (like Shopify, WooCommerce) with inventory systems and automates order processing.

2. Design Your SaaS or Microservice Architecture

The key to building a successful SaaS product is designing a reliable, scalable, and maintainable system. Here's how to approach it:

- **Core Features:**
  - Build n8n workflows for automation tasks, such as API calls, data transfers, or triggering events based on conditions.
  - Implement a user-friendly dashboard for clients to monitor workflows, run reports, and manage automations.
- **User Authentication:**
  - Implement user authentication (e.g., OAuth, JWT) to allow users to securely log in and access their automation workflows.
- **Webhooks and APIs:**

- Expose certain functionality of your service via APIs or webhooks so users can trigger automation from external systems or integrate your service with their existing platforms.
- **Subscription Model:**
  - Offer tiered pricing models, with different levels of access based on the number of workflows, integrations, or automations a user can create.
- **Hosting and Infrastructure:**
  - Use cloud services (e.g., AWS, Google Cloud, Azure) to host your application, ensuring scalability and reliability. Leverage n8n's Dockerized environment for easy deployment.

3. Build and Launch

- **Prototype and MVP:**
  Start by building a minimum viable product (MVP) with core features that demonstrate the value of your service. This allows you to test the market and gather feedback from early users.
- **Iterate Based on Feedback:**
  Collect user feedback, fix bugs, and iterate on the product to make improvements and add new features that customers want.
- **Marketing Your Service:**
  Once you have a working product, create a landing page and start marketing. Highlight how your service solves specific pain points and makes automation easy.
- **Scaling Your Service:**
  As your SaaS or microservice grows, consider implementing additional features like reporting, analytics, and custom integrations to increase value for your users.

14.5 Becoming an n8n Community Influencer

Becoming an influencer in the n8n community can significantly enhance your reputation and open up new monetization opportunities. Influencers in tech communities are recognized for their expertise, engagement, and thought leadership. Here's how you can position yourself as a prominent figure within the n8n ecosystem:

1. Share Knowledge Consistently

The more you contribute to the community, the more visibility you gain. Whether it's through blog posts, tutorials, social media, or answering questions on forums, consistently sharing valuable content will establish you as a go-to expert.

- **Write Tutorials and Guides:**
  Publish detailed guides, how-to articles, and video tutorials on using n8n for various use cases. Make sure to focus on both beginner-friendly and advanced topics to cater to a broader audience.
- **Create Open-Source Projects:**
  Share n8n workflows, templates, and integrations on GitHub or the n8n community forum. The open-source community highly values contributors who share practical, reusable resources.
- **Participate in Online Communities:**
  Join the n8n Discord, forums, Slack channels, or Reddit threads. Actively answer questions, troubleshoot problems, and help others by sharing your experiences.

2. Build Your Personal Brand

To stand out, it's crucial to cultivate a unique personal brand. This brand should reflect your expertise, interests, and approach to automation.

- **Define Your Niche:**
  Decide on a specific area where you want to focus your efforts—whether it's building SaaS products with n8n, creating advanced workflows for business automation, or teaching new users. This niche will help you target the right audience and gain traction.
- **Leverage Social Media:**
  Platforms like LinkedIn, Twitter, and YouTube are great for building your presence. Post tips, tricks, success stories, and video tutorials to engage with the n8n community. Use hashtags like #n8n, #no-code, and #automation to increase visibility.
- **Create a Consistent Content Strategy:**
  Regularly post blogs, videos, or podcasts showcasing your knowledge of n8n and its potential for automation. Maintain a regular schedule to keep your audience engaged.
- **Collaborate with Other Influencers:**
  Partner with other influencers in the no-code, automation, or SaaS space to co-create content, host webinars, or run live Q&A sessions. This will help you expand your network and audience.

3. Host Webinars and Live Sessions

Hosting live webinars or sessions is a great way to engage with your audience and demonstrate your expertise.

- **Teach n8n in Real-Time:**
  Conduct live demonstrations on how to build workflows, automate processes, and integrate n8n with other platforms. Interactive sessions allow viewers to ask questions, making them more valuable.

- **Join or Host n8n Events:**
  Attend or organize community events, workshops, or hackathons. These events provide an opportunity to showcase your skills while networking with other developers and business owners.
- **Offer Q&A Sessions:**
  Host open Q&A sessions where you solve real-world problems with n8n workflows, offering insight into common challenges and automation best practices.

4. Contribute to n8n's Development

Another way to stand out in the community is by contributing to the n8n platform itself.

- **Build Custom Nodes or Plugins:**
  If you have development experience, consider building custom nodes or plugins to extend n8n's functionality. Contributing code or integrating new services can give you recognition within the n8n community.
- **Report Bugs and Feature Requests:**
  Actively participate in n8n's GitHub repository by reporting bugs, submitting feature requests, or reviewing pull requests. Engaging with the technical side of the platform can help you gain respect from other community members and n8n's core team.
- **Collaborate with n8n's Team:**
  Reach out to the n8n team to collaborate on joint initiatives, such as writing content, building tutorials, or presenting at events. As an influencer, your involvement will help promote both your personal brand and n8n.

5. Engage in Content Creation and Sponsorships

As you grow your influence, you can secure partnerships and sponsorships that benefit both your personal brand and the wider community.

- **Sponsor Content:**
  Partner with n8n-related projects or events to sponsor content, tutorials, or workshops. This sponsorship can include video tutorials, blog posts, or webinar hosting.
- **Affiliate Marketing for n8n-related Services:**
  If n8n partners with third-party services (like cloud hosting, API services, or SaaS tools), you can promote these services through affiliate links and earn commissions while providing valuable resources to your community.

14.6 Case Studies: Successful n8n Freelancers and Entrepreneurs

Several freelancers and entrepreneurs have successfully monetized their n8n skills, turning their knowledge into profitable ventures. Here are a few real-world case studies that illustrate different paths to success:

1. Freelancing with n8n Automation

Case Study: Emily, Freelance Workflow Consultant

- **Background:**
  Emily is a freelance consultant specializing in automation for small businesses. After learning n8n, she started offering workflow automation services to local businesses, helping them save time and reduce manual processes.
- **Business Model:**
  Emily offers personalized workflow development, helping businesses integrate n8n with their existing tools like CRMs, email marketing platforms, and social media channels. She charges hourly or project-based rates, depending on the complexity of the automation.
- **Success:**
  Emily has grown her business by focusing on client-specific automation solutions and has developed a reputation for delivering cost-effective and scalable automation processes. Her client base has expanded globally due to her ability to create tailor-made solutions with n8n.

2. Building SaaS Products with n8n

Case Study: Mark, Founder of Automated Reporting SaaS

- **Background:**
  Mark, a seasoned developer, saw the potential of n8n in automating reporting tasks for businesses. He combined his coding skills with n8n's capabilities to create a SaaS product that automatically generates customized reports for businesses based on their data sources.
- **Business Model:**
  Mark offers a subscription-based service where businesses can sign up to automate their reporting tasks. His platform integrates with multiple data sources (Google Sheets, SQL databases, etc.) and generates periodic reports sent via email or Slack.
- **Success:**
  Mark's SaaS platform has grown steadily, with several clients using the service to streamline their reporting workflows. He leverages n8n's scalability to ensure that the platform can handle increasing data volumes as the customer base grows. Mark has been

able to scale the business by focusing on customer feedback and continually improving the product's features.

3. Educating and Mentoring with n8n

Case Study: Sarah, n8n Educator and Online Course Creator

- **Background:**
  Sarah, an experienced automation expert, started creating n8n-related educational content, such as video tutorials, courses, and blog posts. She saw a gap in the market for comprehensive, easy-to-understand training for n8n.
- **Business Model:**
  Sarah monetizes her educational content by offering paid online courses and tutorials on platforms like Udemy and Teachable. She also runs a Patreon page where subscribers can access exclusive lessons, one-on-one sessions, and special community events.
- **Success:**
  Sarah's courses have gained popularity among beginners and intermediate users. Her ability to break down complex concepts into digestible lessons has earned her a loyal following. In addition to course sales, Sarah earns revenue through affiliate marketing for n8n-related tools and services.

4. n8n as a Tool for Business Automation

Case Study: John, Founder of a Marketing Automation Agency

- **Background:**
  John runs a marketing automation agency, offering workflow automation solutions for digital marketing agencies. He uses n8n to integrate marketing tools (e.g., email, CRM, social media) and automate lead generation, nurturing, and follow-up processes.
- **Business Model:**
  John provides end-to-end marketing automation services, from workflow creation to ongoing support and optimization. He offers custom solutions for clients in the digital marketing space, helping them save time and improve campaign efficiency.
- **Success:**
  John's business has thrived due to his ability to automate complex marketing tasks using n8n. His agency works with a range of clients, from startups to large corporations, enabling them to streamline marketing processes while reducing manual labor. He has expanded his service offerings to include marketing analytics and performance tracking.

Chapter 15: Collaboration & Team Automation

As your workflows and automation processes grow, working in teams becomes essential. This chapter will explore how to leverage n8n for team collaboration, focusing on role management, permissions, and best practices for team environments.

15.1 Role Management and Permissions

In team environments, it's crucial to manage who can access, modify, and execute workflows, especially as organizations scale. n8n offers several features to control access, permissions, and roles to ensure that sensitive data is protected and workflows are used appropriately.

1. Understanding User Roles in n8n

n8n allows you to manage user access at different levels. By defining roles and setting permissions, you can control who in your team can create, edit, view, or execute workflows.

- **Admin:**
  Admin users have full access to all workflows, credentials, and system settings. They can add or remove users, configure system-wide settings, and manage permissions for other users.

- **User:**
  Regular users can create, edit, and execute workflows but cannot modify system settings or manage users. Their permissions are generally restricted to workflow management and automation tasks.

- **Viewer:**
  A Viewer role is typically limited to viewing workflows and data but cannot edit or execute them. This role is ideal for stakeholders or clients who need to monitor workflows without making any changes.

2. Creating and Managing Roles

To create and manage roles in n8n:

1. **Access the Settings:**
   Navigate to the admin panel where roles and permissions are configured. This is typically found under **Settings > Users & Permissions**.

2. **Create a New Role:**
   You can create a new role based on your team's needs. Assign permissions for creating, editing, viewing, and executing workflows, as well as accessing other system settings.

3. **Assign Permissions:**
   For each role, you can granularly manage what the user is allowed to do. You can set permissions for:
   - **Workflow Creation:** Whether a user can create new workflows.
   - **Workflow Editing:** Whether a user can modify existing workflows.
   - **Workflow Execution:** Whether a user can trigger workflows manually or automatically.
   - **Viewing Logs & Data:** Whether a user can view execution logs, data input/output, and other workflow-related information.

4. **Assign Users to Roles:**
   Once roles are defined, assign users to specific roles based on their responsibilities. Users can have one or more roles depending on the tasks they need to perform.

5. **Audit Logs:**
   n8n allows administrators to access audit logs to track user activity within the system. These logs can show changes made to workflows, access to sensitive data, and user actions, providing accountability in team environments.

3. Role-Based Access Control (RBAC) for Enhanced Security

Role-Based Access Control (RBAC) ensures that users have access to the specific data and workflows they need without over-privileging them. For example, some users may only need to view workflow data, while others may need full editing and execution permissions.

- **Granular Permissions:** With n8n's role management system, you can assign permissions at a very granular level, such as restricting access to certain workflows, API credentials, or integrations.
- **Audit and Track Permissions:** By auditing permissions and user roles regularly, you can ensure that no one has excessive access, and teams follow the principle of least privilege.

15.2 Using n8n in Team Environments

As businesses grow, automation becomes a collaborative process. When multiple team members work on workflows or integrate automation into larger systems, the ability to collaborate effectively is essential. n8n offers several features and strategies to optimize team workflows and encourage collaboration.

1. Sharing Workflows Across Teams

n8n allows for easy sharing of workflows, both within teams and with external stakeholders.

- **Exporting and Importing Workflows:**
  You can export workflows as JSON files and share them across different team environments or with external partners. These workflows can then be imported into another n8n instance.
- **Template Sharing:**
  n8n also allows the creation of reusable workflow templates. These templates can be shared with the community or kept within your team for recurring automation tasks.
- **Shared Folders:**
  For teams with multiple workflows, shared folders within the n8n instance can organize workflows based on departments, projects, or workflows with common integrations.

2. Collaboration via Workflow Comments and Documentation

Collaboration isn't just about building workflows together—communication and documentation are key components.

- **Commenting on Workflows:**
  n8n allows users to add comments to workflows. This feature can be particularly helpful in a team setting, where developers, automation specialists, or stakeholders can leave notes about what a workflow does, why certain decisions were made, or where to find relevant documentation.
- **Version Control and Documentation:**
  For teams working on complex workflows, having version control and documentation is crucial. Maintain a changelog to document all modifications to workflows, their triggers, and associated integrations.
- **Collaborative Testing:**
  When workflows are created or modified, team members can test the workflow together to ensure it performs as expected. Assign roles within the team to test different parts of the workflow, especially for large automation systems involving multiple steps and integrations.

3. Using n8n for Cross-Department Automation

In many organizations, workflows can span across multiple departments or teams. n8n makes it easy to collaborate between different departments such as marketing, sales, support, and operations.

- **Sales and Marketing Alignment:**
  Integrating tools like CRM systems (e.g., Salesforce) and email platforms (e.g., Mailchimp) within n8n can streamline workflows between sales and marketing teams. This enables seamless lead generation, nurturing, and reporting across teams.
- **Operations and Support Collaboration:**
  Support teams can benefit from n8n automations that pull data from helpdesk systems (e.g., Zendesk) or inventory management tools (e.g., Airtable). Operations can use n8n to automate processes such as order fulfillment or stock management, all while staying aligned with the support team's needs.

4. Real-Time Collaboration with n8n's Webhooks

Using webhooks, n8n can trigger real-time updates between teams working on different aspects of the workflow.

- **Immediate Action Triggers:**
  A webhook can be set up to trigger a workflow in real time based on certain actions in external systems. For example, when a support ticket is created, a webhook could automatically update the sales team's dashboard or notify the relevant team members to respond to customer inquiries.
- **External System Synchronization:**
  Teams can stay in sync by leveraging n8n's webhook feature to communicate between various systems in real-time. For example, a marketing team can trigger a campaign workflow automatically when a new lead is added to a CRM.

5. Scaling Team Workflows

As your team grows, n8n can scale with your organization, helping you manage more complex and high-volume automation tasks.

- **Sub-Workflows for Modular Collaboration:**
  n8n allows you to create sub-workflows, which are smaller, modular workflows that can be reused within other workflows. This reduces duplication of effort and allows different team members to focus on building specific sub-workflows. The main workflow can pull these sub-workflows together, creating a cohesive system of automation.
- **Performance and Monitoring for Team Environments:**
  Monitoring and tracking the performance of workflows in team environments is essential to ensure optimal efficiency. n8n's built-in execution logs, along with third-party integrations, can help track workflow performance, making it easier to identify bottlenecks and areas for improvement.

15.3 Automating Across Multiple Users

As teams adopt automation for routine operations, one common requirement is enabling workflows to operate **on behalf of multiple users**—either to perform tasks under different credentials, or to dynamically adapt logic based on the user involved. This is critical for organizations managing shared processes, like CRM updates, multi-user content pipelines, or approval systems.

1. Why Multi-User Automation Matters

Automating across multiple users allows a single workflow to:

- Perform tasks for multiple team members (e.g., send daily reports to each salesperson).
- Access external services using **user-specific tokens** or credentials.
- Route tasks dynamically (e.g., assign a support ticket to the right agent).
- Handle approval workflows where **different users act at different stages**.

2. Techniques for Multi-User Automation in n8n

There are several ways to implement this functionality in n8n depending on the use case:

A. Dynamic Credential Usage

If each user has their own set of credentials (e.g., Gmail OAuth tokens), n8n allows workflows to dynamically choose which credential to use.

- **How it works:**
  Use a Set or Function node to assign a value to a field like user_id, and reference the correct credential in an API or email node using **expressions**.

Example:

```
{{$json["user_gmail_credential_id"]}}
```

- In this case, the Gmail node dynamically uses the credential ID stored in the data for that specific user.
- **Use Cases:**
  - Sending personalized emails from a user's own Gmail account.
  - Making API requests with a user's access token.
  - Uploading files to the right cloud storage location for each user.

B. Iterating Over Users (Loops)

Use the **SplitInBatches** node to loop over a list of users, performing actions for each one.

- **Step-by-step:**
    1. Retrieve a list of users from a database or Airtable.
    2. Use SplitInBatches to iterate over them.
    3. For each user, perform the required tasks: send a message, create a report, update CRM, etc.
- **Bonus:** You can parallelize execution using sub-workflows to improve performance.

C. Workflow Trigger Based on User Context

When using Webhooks or internal API endpoints, pass a **user ID or token** in the payload to identify which user the workflow should act on behalf of.

- **Security Note:** Always validate and sanitize incoming data to prevent misuse or impersonation.

D. Multi-Step, Multi-User Workflows

n8n can support approval workflows involving multiple people:

- **Example:** A document approval system.
    1. Document is uploaded.
    2. Reviewer A is notified and must approve.
    3. If approved, Reviewer B is notified.
    4. On full approval, the document is processed.

Use IF, Wait, and Webhook nodes to build these asynchronous, stateful processes across users.

3. Handling User-Specific Data and Security

To protect user data while automating across multiple identities:

- **Isolate credentials**: Store them securely using the built-in **Credential Manager**.
- **Use environment variables**: For access tokens, API keys, and permission scopes.
- **Audit logs**: Enable execution logs to track workflow actions per user.
- **Conditional branching**: Add checks to ensure users only access what they're authorized to.

15.4 Workflow Sharing and Collaboration Tools

Beyond user-level automation, n8n enables teams to **collaborate effectively** when designing, managing, and deploying workflows. In this section, we'll cover tools, strategies, and best practices for workflow collaboration.

1. Shared Workflow Spaces

In self-hosted and enterprise setups, you can create **shared folders or spaces**:

- Organize workflows by department or project (e.g., "Marketing", "Ops").
- Manage access control per folder or workflow.
- Improve discovery and reuse of workflows by teammates.

2. Exporting and Importing Workflows

n8n supports full export/import functionality:

- **Export:** Click the "Download" button on any workflow to save a .json file.
- **Import:** Use the "Import Workflow" button to load it into any n8n instance.

This makes it easy to:

- Share workflows between team members.
- Backup and version-control workflows in Git.
- Publish reusable templates for clients or open-source sharing.

3. Collaborative Documentation

Workflows should be self-explanatory to improve team efficiency. Use these tools:

- **Notes and Comments:** Add notes directly to nodes to explain their purpose.
- **Naming conventions:** Use consistent and clear names for workflows, nodes, and credentials.
- **Workflow descriptions:** Fill in the description field for each workflow to explain its goal and integration points.

4. Git Integration for Workflow Versioning

While n8n doesn't have native Git integration out of the box, you can:

- Store workflow .json files in a Git repo.
- Use pre-deployment hooks or CI pipelines to import workflows to staging/production environments.

- Track changes, handle pull requests, and review updates collaboratively.

For enterprise workflows, consider building a DevOps pipeline around your n8n deployments.

5. Using the n8n Community for Collaboration

n8n has an active community forum and marketplace where teams can:

- Share workflows, nodes, or plugins.
- Collaborate on best practices.
- Get feedback on solutions and discuss automation challenges.

15.5 Governance Best Practices

As n8n becomes a central tool for automation in teams or organizations, implementing governance is critical to ensure security, maintainability, scalability, and compliance. Without it, workflows can become fragile, inconsistent, and hard to manage—especially in environments with multiple users or contributors.

This section outlines **best practices** for governing your n8n workflows and infrastructure, particularly in **team-based or enterprise** deployments.

1. Role-Based Access Control (RBAC)

Implement RBAC to define **who can do what** within the platform.

- **User Roles** should include:
  - **Admins**: Full access to all workflows, credentials, and settings.
  - **Developers**: Can create and edit workflows, but not change sensitive credentials.
  - **Viewers/Operators**: Can trigger and monitor workflows, but not modify them.
- **Best Practices:**
  - Use **least privilege** principles.
  - Regularly audit roles and permissions.
  - Use **environment-specific roles** (e.g., different roles for staging vs production).

2. Credential and Secret Management

Credentials are the lifeblood of workflow automation and must be governed tightly.

- **Store credentials** in n8n's built-in credential manager or use a secure secret manager (e.g., Vault, AWS Secrets Manager).
- **Never hard-code** tokens, passwords, or API keys directly in nodes or expressions.
- **Use environment variables** to store instance-wide secrets.

- **Rotate credentials** regularly and automatically when possible.

3. Workflow Naming and Documentation Standards

Clear, consistent naming conventions and in-flow documentation help teams understand and maintain automation.

- **Use consistent naming:**
  team-process-action, e.g., marketing-slack-daily-summary.
- **Add metadata and descriptions** to workflows:
  - Purpose of the workflow.
  - Input and output structure.
  - External systems involved.
- **Use Node Notes** and comments to explain complex logic.

4. Workflow Lifecycle Management

Automations should follow a clear development-to-deployment pipeline.

- **Use environments**:
  Separate workflows into **development**, **staging**, and **production** environments.
- **Version workflows**:
  - Tag and backup stable workflow versions.
  - Use Git or CI pipelines to deploy .json exports into controlled environments.
- **Approval workflows** for deployment:
  - Require code review or testing before deploying to production.

5. Auditing and Logging

Enable and monitor logs to maintain accountability and traceability.

- **Execution Logs**: Regularly audit for failures, anomalies, or unexpected behaviors.
- **Credential Access Logs**: Monitor who accessed or modified secrets.
- **User Activity Logs**: Track who changed workflows and when.

For high-security environments, **export logs to SIEM** systems for analysis and alerting.

6. Data Privacy and Compliance

Workflows often process sensitive or regulated data (e.g., PII, financial data).

- **Anonymize or mask sensitive data** in logs and exports.
- **Encrypt sensitive fields** using platform-level encryption or external services.
- Ensure workflows comply with **GDPR, HIPAA, SOC2**, or other relevant standards.

- **Data retention policies**: Clean up temporary or stored data at appropriate intervals.

7. Monitoring and Alerting

Governance also involves proactive monitoring.

- **Set up alerting** for:
  - Failed workflows.
  - Long-running executions.
  - Threshold-based alerts (e.g., too many API calls).
- Use tools like:
  - **Prometheus + Grafana** for custom metrics.
  - **Third-party APM tools** for external visibility.

8. Template and Sub-Workflow Governance

Prevent duplication and enforce standardization by governing shared templates.

- Maintain a **central template library**.
- Enforce reviews before adding shared templates.
- Use **sub-workflows** for repeated tasks (e.g., sending emails, logging errors).

9. Change Management and Collaboration Policy

- Use **pull requests** or ticketing systems to review workflow changes.
- Document changes and rationales.
- Use changelogs or workflow description fields to communicate updates.

Governance Checklist

Area	Best Practice	Tool/Feature to Use
Access Control	Role-based access	n8n user roles
Credential Handling	Use secure storage, rotate regularly	Credential Manager, .env

Workflow Hygiene	Clear names, metadata, and documentation	Descriptions, Node Notes
Lifecycle Management	Dev → Stage → Prod flow	Git, CI/CD, Environments
Logging & Auditing	Track user actions and errors	Execution Logs, External Logs
Compliance	Encrypt, anonymize, and retain wisely	Environment Configs
Monitoring	Alerts and dashboards for reliability	Prometheus, Webhooks
Template Management	Central library and usage rules	Workflow Templates

Chapter 16: Productivity Boosters & Workflow Hacks

Building automations is powerful—but building them efficiently is transformational. This chapter focuses on tips, tricks, and tools that dramatically increase your productivity, help you avoid repetition, and maintain clean, scalable workflows. Whether you're a solo builder or part of a team, these strategies will help you get more done in less time with n8n.

16.1 Keyboard Shortcuts & UI Tips

Efficiency in n8n isn't just about building workflows—it's also about navigating and using the interface like a pro. This section introduces **keyboard shortcuts, UI enhancements, and time-saving habits** that boost your workflow creation speed.

1. Essential Keyboard Shortcuts in n8n

Shortcut (Windows/Linux)	Shortcut (macOS)	Action
Ctrl + Click	Cmd + Click	Multi-select nodes
Ctrl + C / V	Cmd + C / V	Copy and paste selected nodes
Ctrl + Z / Y	Cmd + Z / Y	Undo / Redo
Delete	Delete	Delete selected node(s)
Esc	Esc	Close open dialog or cancel action

Tab	Tab	Switch between input fields

Tip: When copying nodes, the connections between them are preserved if copied together.

2. Canvas Navigation & Layout Tricks

- **Drag to Pan**: Click and drag anywhere on the canvas to move around.
- **Zoom In/Out**: Use mouse scroll or Ctrl + +/- to zoom.
- **Reset View**: Use the zoom control button in the lower-right corner to reset canvas focus.
- **Organize with Comments**: Use the **Sticky Notes** node to label sections of your workflow.
- **Align Nodes**: Manually align or use grid snapping to keep your layout tidy.

3. Node Management Best Practices

- **Use the "Set" node** early** to clean or shape your data** before branching.
- **Color-code nodes**: Though not native yet, using a naming convention or comment nodes with colored emojis (●, □) can simulate visual grouping.
- **Label every IF/Switch** node clearly** with what condition it checks.

4. Search & Navigation Hacks

- **Global Search (Cmd/Ctrl + F)**: Search for nodes by name in the workflow canvas.
- **Node Type Search**: When adding a node, use keywords like "webhook", "function", or service names.
- **Minimap Use**: Enable minimap from the settings (if available) to navigate large workflows.

5. Efficiency Habits

- **Clone workflows** to create variations quickly.
- **Use pinned expressions** to test variables on the fly.
- **Run individual nodes** during development to avoid executing the full flow.

16.2 Git for Workflow Management

Version control is essential for professional development. While n8n doesn't natively integrate Git, you can still manage workflows using Git-friendly practices.

1. Why Use Git with n8n?

- **Track changes over time**
- **Collaborate across teams**
- **Rollback to earlier versions**
- **Maintain clean audit trails**

2. Exporting and Importing Workflows

- Export from n8n UI as .json files:
  - Menu → **Export** → "Download Workflow"
- Save these files in a Git repo (e.g., workflows/marketing/slack-daily-summary.json)
- Use Git for:
  - **Branching workflows**
  - **Pull requests for updates**
  - **Release tagging**

3. Folder Structure Recommendations

/workflows/

└── marketing/

├── slack-daily-summary.json

└── email-welcome-series.json

└── sales/

└── crm-lead-capture.json

/scripts/

.env.example

README.md

Include a README.md to describe each folder's purpose and setup instructions.

4. Syncing with GitHub Actions or CI/CD

While manual import/export works for smaller teams, large teams can automate:

- Auto-deploy .json files to n8n via **n8n CLI** or **API**
- Validate changes through **CI/CD pipelines**

- Use GitHub Actions to trigger workflows or backups on pushes

Example CI step:

```
- name: Deploy n8n Workflow

  run: n8n import:workflow --input=./workflows/marketing/slack-daily-summary.json
```

5. Git Ignore and Security

Never commit .env files or credentials.

Add this to .gitignore:

```
.env

secrets/

node_modules/

credentials.json
```

16.3 Common Automation Patterns

Mastering a few key patterns will drastically increase your efficiency and reduce the risk of error in n8n. These reusable "automation blueprints" can be applied across projects and industries.

1. Trigger + API Call + Notification

Use Case: New lead form → Slack notification
Pattern:

- **Webhook or Form Trigger**
- **HTTP Request to CRM**
- **Slack/Email/Discord Notification**

[Webhook Trigger] → [HTTP Node (CRM API)] → [Slack Node]

2. Scheduled Data Sync

Use Case: Nightly sync of Airtable and Google Sheets
Pattern:

- **Cron Node**
- **Source API**

- **Destination API**
- **Optional: Merge or Deduplicate Node**

[Cron] → [HTTP Request] → [Merge] → [Google Sheets]

3. Data Classification with AI

Use Case: Classify customer support tickets
 Pattern:

- **Webhook Trigger or Polling**
- **OpenAI/Claude Node**
- **Switch/IF Node for Routing**

[Webhook] → [OpenAI] → [IF] → [Route to Slack/Email/CRM]

4. Error Notification Wrapper

Use Case: Alert on failures
 Pattern:

- **Try block**
- **Catch block → Notify**

[Main Workflow Logic]

↓

[Error Trigger]

↓

[Slack/Email: Error Details]

5. Approval Workflow

Use Case: Approve new content/posts/tasks
 Pattern:

- **Trigger**
- **Wait Node (for user input or manual Slack button)**
- **Conditional logic**

[Trigger] → [Send for Approval] → [Wait] → [IF: Approved?]

16.4 Testing Automation Before Production

Launching an untested workflow in production can be risky. Here's how to test smartly.

Best Practices

1. **Use a Sandbox Dataset**
   - Clone production data to a test table or spreadsheet.
   - Use mock API endpoints or httpbin.org.
2. **Enable Manual Execution**
   - Run nodes one-by-one.
   - Watch the data as it flows and check node outputs.
3. **Use Static Input (Set Node)**
   - Simulate payloads instead of triggering from live sources.

[Set Node: Sample Data] → [Downstream Logic]

4. **Activate Execution Logs**

   - Monitor status, errors, and retries under *Executions* tab.
   - Store logs externally via webhook or database for auditing.

5. **Use Conditional Testing Flags**
   - Include a toggle variable (test_mode=true) in the flow.
   - Send outputs to test channels or folders if flag is active.

[IF: test_mode?] → [Slack-Test] / [Slack-Prod]

Mocking External Services

- Use tools like **Mocky.io**, **Beeceptor**, or **Webhook.site** to simulate responses.
- Useful for retry scenarios, error-handling, and integration tests.

Version Control for Safety

- Keep separate **dev** and **prod** workflow copies.
- Use .env.dev and .env.prod files to isolate credentials and URLs.

16.5 Creating a Personal Automation Dashboard

A personal automation dashboard built with n8n empowers you to monitor, control, and visualize your workflows—all in one place. It can include stats, logs, quick-action triggers, and links to your most-used automations.

Benefits of a Dashboard

- One-click access to trigger workflows manually
- Centralized overview of logs, errors, and task counts
- Embedded metrics (e.g., number of emails sent, leads added)
- Easier debugging and monitoring across workflows

Building Blocks of a Personal Dashboard

1. Trigger Panel

Goal: Manually start commonly used workflows
Components:

- **Webhook Nodes** acting as trigger endpoints
- A simple **HTML frontend** with buttons linked to these endpoints

Example:

```
<button onclick="fetch('https://your-n8n-instance/webhook/email_report')">Send Email Report</button>
```

2. Live Stats and Counters

Goal: Display real-time workflow metrics
Pattern:

- **Cron Node** (e.g., every hour)
- **Query DB/API**
- **Set Node to format**
- **Send to Google Sheets/Notion/Custom frontend**

Example Metrics:

Workflow	Count (Last 24h)
Invoices Sent	25
New Leads Captured	18
Errors Logged	2

3. Execution Logs and Error Summary

Goal: View success/failure stats
Pattern:

- Use n8n's **Execution List API**
- Parse recent runs
- Send summary to Notion, Slack, or a dashboard frontend

[Cron] → [HTTP (n8n API)] → [Filter by Status] → [Format for Display]

4. Quick Access Links

Goal: Add links to open or clone workflows
Method:

- Include direct URLs to n8n workflow IDs
- Optionally embed in Notion, a dashboard app (e.g., Retool), or your local HTML file

```
<a href="https://n8n.io/workflow/23">View Email Automation</a>
```

5. Alerts and Notifications

Goal: Display or send alerts if something breaks
Pattern:

- Use IF nodes to detect errors
- Route to Slack, Email, or on-dashboard notification system

Tools for Dashboard Frontends

Tool	Use Case	Pros
Notion	Embedded tables/stats	Easy to update & access
Google Sheets	Live sync with metrics	Charts, filters, permissions
Custom HTML	Fully customizable dashboard	Buttons, graphs, AJAX updates
Retool/Appsmith	Pro dashboards	Integrated APIs, auth, charts

Example Use Case

Daily Automation Summary Email Dashboard

- Cron triggers at 8:00 AM
- Collects yesterday's data from various workflows
- Formats into an email template
- Sends to yourself or a small team

Best Practices

- Group workflows by **category** (e.g., marketing, dev ops, personal)
- Use **consistent webhook naming** (dashboard_trigger_send_invoice)
- Add **authentication** if exposing triggers publicly
- Back up your dashboard configuration and links

Chapter 17: What's New & What's Next in n8n

As n8n continues to evolve, staying informed about the latest features and future roadmap is essential for maintaining cutting-edge automations. This chapter provides an overview of recent updates, ongoing trends, and anticipated developments in the n8n ecosystem.

17.1 Latest Features and Community Nodes

As n8n evolves, it regularly introduces powerful new features while fostering a vibrant ecosystem of community contributions. This section highlights recent **core features**, enhancements to the **user experience**, and standout **community-built nodes** that have expanded n8n's capabilities.

Latest Core Features (2024–2025)

Here are some of the most impactful features introduced in recent n8n releases:

Feature	Description	Benefit
Credential Encryption Vault	Improved secure credential storage with encryption-at-rest	Enterprise-grade security
Custom Variables Panel	Allows persistent, global, and workflow-level variables	Easier reusability and cleaner logic
Error Workflow Handling	Global error workflows that trigger on failure across all workflows	Centralized failure management

FunctionItem Improvements	Enhanced loop capabilities, access to context and metadata	More powerful custom logic
Built-in OpenAI Node (Official)	First-party support for ChatGPT, completions, and embeddings	Faster AI integration
Dynamic Expressions Debugger	Real-time preview of expression output before execution	Easier testing and troubleshooting
Team Projects (n8n Cloud)	Dedicated spaces for teams to manage workflows with access control	Collaboration and organization

Popular Community Nodes

The community continues to innovate by building custom nodes for niche and advanced integrations. Here are some highly useful and trending community nodes:

Community Node	Purpose/Use Case	Author/Source
Telegram Bot Advanced	Enhanced Telegram bot controls	@SvenPet
Google Ads Node	Automate ad campaign reporting and optimization	Community

Notion Database Tools	Deep integration with Notion databases	Community/Marketplace
Zoho CRM Node	Manage leads, deals, and contacts via Zoho	Community contributor
Plausible Analytics	Fetch traffic data from privacy-friendly analytics	Marketplace
Cloudinary	Image hosting and transformation workflows	Community node pack

You can install community nodes via the **n8n Marketplace**, accessible directly from the UI or CLI.

Where to Discover New Nodes

- **n8n Marketplace**: Integrated directly into n8n UI
- n8n.io/nodes: Full searchable listing
- **GitHub Community Projects**: Open-source contributions to fork and adapt
- **Forum & Discord**: Announcements and beta releases often appear here first

17.2 The n8n Roadmap

The future of n8n is shaped by its open-source community and core team, with an emphasis on **scalability, AI assistance, developer experience, and enterprise collaboration**.

Short-Term Roadmap (0–6 Months)

Planned Feature	Description	Status
Workflow Collaboration Tools	Real-time commenting, changelog view	In Development

AI-Assisted Workflow Creation	Suggest nodes/logic using prompts and AI	In Beta
Enhanced Scheduler UI	Visual time picker, timezone handling	Planned
Web UI Theming	Light/dark mode, customizable node colors	Planned
Node Version Pinning	Lock workflows to specific node versions	Under Review

Mid-Term Roadmap (6–12 Months)

Feature	Description	Potential Benefit
Advanced Error Routing UI	Drag-and-drop error handlers and fallback paths	Better reliability for critical flows
Built-in Git Integration	Pull/push workflows to Git repositories directly	Native version control
Mobile App or Interface	View, trigger, or monitor workflows via mobile	On-the-go workflow management
Enterprise Metrics Dashboard	Central logging, success/failure ratios, graphs	Operational transparency

How to Stay Informed

- n8n Roadmap Page

- **GitHub Project Tracker**: View issues, milestones, and pull requests
- **Release Notes on Blog**: https://n8n.io/blog

- **Community Forum Announcements**
- **@n8n_io Twitter / LinkedIn for real-time updates**

Key Takeaways

- n8n's development is active and community-driven, with major innovations happening regularly.
- Keeping up with new features and community nodes ensures you're building with the best tools available.
- The future of n8n includes deeper AI integration, real-time collaboration, and Git-native workflows—making it even more powerful for teams and developers.

17.3 Upcoming Node Ideas and Opportunities

As n8n continues to grow, the opportunity to create **custom nodes**—either for personal use or to share with the community—is greater than ever. With thousands of SaaS tools and APIs available, there's a huge gap in automation coverage that creative developers and no-code builders can fill.

Emerging Areas Ripe for Node Development

Category	Node Ideas	Opportunity Level
AI & LLMs	Claude, Gemini, Perplexity, LLaMA APIs	Very High
E-Commerce	WooCommerce, BigCommerce, Printful, Etsy	High

Marketing	ActiveCampaign, Instapage, Kartra	High
CRM & Sales	Close.io, Pipedrive, Copper CRM	Medium
Analytics & SEO	Ahrefs, Semrush, Fathom Analytics	Medium
Finance & Payments	Wise, QuickBooks, FreshBooks	Medium
HR & Recruiting	Workable, BambooHR, Greenhouse	Niche Growth
IoT / Smart Devices	Home Assistant, Tuya API, SmartThings	Emerging
Crypto & Web3	Alchemy, Moralis, MetaMask, OpenSea	Emerging

Tip: Browse RapidAPI or APIs.guru for ideas on APIs to wrap in new nodes.

Opportunities for Builders

- **Fill Gaps in the Marketplace**: Many APIs still lack nodes. Adding them gives you visibility and credibility.
- **Build Micro-products**: You can monetize niche nodes (e.g., Premium e-commerce integrations).
- **Collaborate with Brands**: Offer to build official n8n nodes for growing SaaS startups.
- **Use It in Your Portfolio**: Great way to demonstrate technical + no-code skills.

Tools to Help Build Nodes Faster

- n8n-node-dev CLI
- Node template generators (npx create-n8n-node)
- Node starter repositories on GitHub
- n8n Community Dev Channel (Discord)

17.4 Keeping Up with Weekly Releases

n8n follows a **fast and frequent release cycle**, often pushing updates **weekly**. Staying updated ensures you're using the most efficient and secure tools available in the platform.

Release Schedule and Channels

Release Type	Frequency	Includes
Stable	Weekly	Core features, fixes, node updates
Beta/Canary	Ad hoc	Experimental tools, pre-release nodes
Community Nodes	Continuous	Marketplace submissions and approvals

How to Stay Updated

Channel	Content	Link
Changelog Page	Weekly release notes & patch logs	n8n.io/changelog

GitHub Releases	Source-level details, tags	GitHub Repo
n8n Blog	Feature deep-dives, use cases	n8n Blog
Discord Community	Early announcements & beta testing	n8n Discord
Twitter & LinkedIn	Social media updates	@n8n_io

Recommended Workflow to Stay Current

1. Subscribe to GitHub releases (watch → custom → releases)

2. Join the #announcements channel on Discord

3. Enable Marketplace auto-update (if available in UI)

4. Periodically check `n8n.io/nodes` for new node categories

5. Review the n8n blog monthly for big-picture trends

Key Takeaways

- There are hundreds of potential nodes yet to be built—both for fun and profit.
- Contributing nodes boosts your profile, improves the ecosystem, and can generate income.
- Weekly releases ensure you're never too far behind; just plug into the right channels.

Chapter 18: Resources and Continuing Your Journey

By this point, you've gained a comprehensive understanding of how to use n8n for everything from basic automations to building robust systems and even monetizing your skills. But the journey doesn't end here. n8n is an evolving platform, and staying connected with resources and the community is essential for continued growth.

18.1 Official Docs, Courses, and YouTube

Official Documentation

The n8n Docs should be your first stop whenever you want:

- Detailed explanations of nodes, triggers, and workflows
- Configuration guides (Cloud, Docker, CLI)
- Advanced topics like credentials, environment variables, and custom nodes

Pro Tip: Bookmark the n8n Cheat Sheet for a quick reference to syntax and common use-cases.

Online Courses & Learning Paths

Here are some curated learning platforms and their offerings:

Platform	Course Name	Skill Level
n8n Academy	Official onboarding & advanced tracks	Beginner–Expert
Udemy	"n8n - Workflow Automation Mastery"	Beginner
YouTube	Official n8n Channel & community tutorials	All Levels

| LinkedIn Learning | General automation concepts (pair with n8n) | Intermediate |

YouTube Channels to Follow

Channel	Focus
n8n.io	Official demos, tutorials, feature launches
Automate All the Things	Real-world n8n use-cases
James Q Quick	No-code + developer automations
Zapsync	SaaS integrations & workflows

18.2 Active Communities and Slack Groups

Staying active in n8n's thriving community can open doors to new opportunities, ideas, and support.

Official n8n Discord Server

- **Link:** discord.gg/n8n

- Channels include:
    - #general – open discussions
    - #workflows – show off what you've built
    - #support – get help from users and devs
    - #community-nodes – talk about node development

Great place to interact with the n8n team directly!

Slack & Niche Communities

While Discord is the official hub, other communities also provide high-value interactions:

Community	Description	Join Link
Makerpad	No-code builders + automation enthusiasts	makerpad.co
Indie Hackers	Entrepreneurs using automation to scale	indiehackers.com
Automation Town	Workflow professionals + tool builders	Invite-only or via Discord links
Reddit r/n8n_io	Community use-cases & scripts	reddit.com/r/n8n_io

n8n Meetups and Hackathons

- **n8n Meetup** events happen both virtually and in-person.
- **Community Hackathons** let you compete, build, and earn recognition.
- Watch the n8n Blog and Discord #events channel for announcements.

Key Takeaways

- Use the **official docs** for deep learning and syntax clarity.
- Subscribe to **YouTube channels** and **learning platforms** for visual and hands-on guidance.
- Join **Discord and niche communities** to get help, collaborate, and stay inspired.
- Contribute back by answering questions, sharing nodes, or writing tutorials.

18.3 Workflow Marketplaces and Templates

Pre-built templates and workflow marketplaces can significantly reduce the time it takes to implement solutions. Whether you're prototyping, building for a client, or scaling automation in production, these resources give you a head start.

Official n8n Workflow Templates

- **Location:** n8n.io/workflows

- Curated and categorized by use-case:
    - **SaaS integrations** (e.g., Slack to Google Sheets)
    - **AI & NLP** (OpenAI summaries, classification)
    - **E-commerce automations**
    - **Marketing workflows**
- Templates are maintained and verified by the n8n team.

Community-Driven Templates

These are workflows shared by individual users and teams:

Source	Description
n8n Community Forum	Users share their real-world use cases
GitHub Repos (e.g., n8n-templates)	Searchable libraries of JSON workflows
n8n Discord #workflows	Live discussion + shared examples
Blog Posts & Tutorials	Many bloggers include downloadable JSONs

Third-Party Marketplaces

Platform	Type	Notes
Gumroad & Ko-fi	Paid/Free workflow packs	Often niche-specific (e.g., real estate CRM)
Awesome-n8n	Curated GitHub list of resources	Includes templates, nodes, guides
Fiverr & Upwork	Freelancers selling templates	Custom-built automations for client workflows

Always inspect third-party templates before using them in production. Ensure sensitive data (like API keys) is removed and flows are compliant with your privacy/security standards.

18.4 Recommended Tools, Books, and Blogs

While n8n is the hub, a great automation stack includes tools that help design, debug, monitor, and extend your workflows.

Useful Tools for n8n Users

Tool	Use Case
Postman	Test API endpoints before adding to n8n
Insomnia	Lightweight API client for REST/GraphQL
Make.com / Zapier	For comparison & hybrid use-cases

Draw.io / Whimsical	Visualize complex workflows
Logtail / Sentry	Monitoring and error logging
n8n CLI	Workflow execution, import/export via terminal
VS Code	JavaScript function editing, .env management

Books to Expand Your Knowledge

Book Title	Topic	Why Read It
Automate the Boring Stuff with Python	General automation (Python)	Pairs well with scripting in n8n
The No-Code Playbook by Creators of Unqork	No-code strategy	Great for positioning n8n in businesses
Building Microservices by Sam Newman	Architecture	Helps when scaling with n8n
The Art of Workflow Automation (online PDF)	Process optimization	Theory + real-life business flows

Top Blogs and Reading Hubs

Blog/Website	Focus
n8n Blog	Feature releases, tutorials, and use cases
The Productivists	No-code automation trends
Better Programming (Medium)	Developer-friendly no-code concepts
Hackernoon Automation	Indie dev & business automation stories
OpenAI Dev Blog	Ideas for AI + workflow automation

Key Takeaways

- Templates accelerate workflow creation—use official and community resources.
- Leverage design, testing, and monitoring tools to work smarter with n8n.
- Broaden your skills by reading industry books and keeping up with niche blogs.
- Always verify and adapt templates to your own needs and security posture.

18.5 Staying Inspired with Automation

Staying inspired is crucial for long-term success with automation—especially in a fast-moving space like no-code. Automation is not just a tool, it's a mindset: finding ways to remove friction, amplify impact, and create smarter systems. In this section, you'll learn how to stay energized, creative, and connected in your automation journey.

Adopt the "Automate First" Mindset

- **Look for patterns** in your daily routine or business workflows. Ask: *Can this be automated or semi-automated?*

- Keep a **"Workflow Wishlist"** in a Notion doc or Trello board where you log repetitive tasks or ideas to automate later.
- Review your processes every quarter to **refactor or enhance existing automations**.

Get Inspired by Others

- **Follow n8n creators** on Twitter, YouTube, and Medium.
- Explore real-world workflows shared in the **n8n community forum** and Discord.
- Subscribe to newsletters like:
  - *No Code Weekly*
  - *n8n Updates*
  - *The Indie Hacker Digest* (often full of automation hacks)

Try Weekly Mini Challenges

Create a habit of experimenting:

Challenge Idea	Tools to Try
Auto-save tweets to Notion	Twitter, Notion, Cron
Daily morning summary to Slack	RSS, Weather API, Slack
AI-assisted journaling	OpenAI, Google Docs
Invoice tracker in Airtable	Stripe, Airtable, Email
Lead enrichment from form data	Typeform, Clearbit, HubSpot

This keeps your skills sharp and builds a portfolio of use cases.

Join the Automation Movement

- **Attend virtual meetups, hackathons, and webinars.**

- Get involved in the **n8n Contributor Program** or write for their blog.
- **Help others in the forum**—explaining solutions builds mastery.
- Teach others! Launch a **YouTube channel**, run workshops, or share workflows on LinkedIn.

Automate for Yourself, Not Just for Work

Some of the most fulfilling automations are personal:

- Track your reading habits or mood
- Automate your digital garden (blog, notes, links)
- Sync memories and journaling with photos or quotes
- Get notified when your favorite author releases a book

Let automation **enhance your life**, not just your productivity.

Key Takeaways

- Inspiration comes from curiosity—observe repetitive patterns and ask, "Can this be automated?"
- Surround yourself with a community of creators, makers, and tinkerers.
- Build in public, teach others, and challenge yourself regularly.
- Let automation serve not just your business goals, but your personal growth too.

Appendices

This section provides quick-access reference material to support your automation work in n8n. These appendices are designed to be concise, solution-oriented, and regularly revisitable as you encounter challenges or need implementation shortcuts.

Appendix A: Common Errors and Fixes

A handy guide to troubleshoot frequent issues encountered in n8n workflows.

Error Message / Symptom	Cause	Fix / Solution
401 Unauthorized or 403 Forbidden	Invalid or missing API key/token	Check credentials, headers, and token format
ENOTFOUND or ECONNREFUSED	Incorrect URL or DNS issue	Double-check API endpoint, URL spelling, or internet connection
"Cannot read property 'xyz' of undefined"	Accessing a missing field in expression	Add checks or use {{$json?.field}} to avoid runtime errors
Unexpected output in a SplitInBatches	Mismatched data structure	Use Set/Function node to format data before batching
Data doesn't show up in next node	Node wasn't connected properly	Ensure all relevant paths are connected visually

Webhook not triggered	Missing credentials or wrong HTTP method	Verify webhook method (POST/GET), URL, and connection settings
Workflow runs too many times	Infinite loop or trigger misconfigured	Add conditions or rate-limiting logic to control execution
Environment variable not loading	Missing in .env file or config	Check .env syntax, restart n8n, and ensure variable exists
Delay/Wait node not working as expected	Execution mode set to manual/test	Test using Production or Queue mode for time-based nodes
OAuth2 callback fails	Redirect URI mismatch or token expired	Double-check the registered redirect URI and token freshness

Tip: Use the **Execution Log** and **"Raw Data"** tab in node output to debug problems quickly.

Appendix B: API Authentication Cheat Sheet

Quick reference for setting up API credentials for the most common authentication types used in n8n.

1. Basic Authentication

Username: your_username

Password: your_password

Use HTTP Request node → Authentication: *Basic Auth*

2. API Key (Header or Query)

Method	Location	How to Set in n8n
Header	x-api-key	Use HTTP node → Headers: x-api-key: VALUE
Query Param	?key=value	Append to URL or use qs property

3. Bearer Token

Authorization: Bearer <token>

Set this in HTTP node headers, or use **Credential Manager** → **HTTP Auth** → Bearer Token.

4. OAuth2

- Requires: Client ID, Client Secret, Callback URL
- Used in: Google APIs, LinkedIn, Microsoft Graph, etc.
- Set in **Credentials**:
    - Auth URI & Token URI
    - Scopes
    - Grant Type: Authorization Code

Note: Ensure redirect URI matches exactly in your app configuration.

5. Custom Auth Workflows

For APIs with unique flows:

- Use a combination of HTTP requests to get the token → Store in static data or environment variables
- Use **Function** or **Set** nodes to inject tokens into headers

Recommended Credential Setup Flow

1. Check API docs: Auth type? Scope? Rate limits?
2. Use Credential Manager in n8n for reusability
3. Store sensitive keys in .env or Secret Manager
4. Test using HTTP Request node with sample endpoint

Appendix C: Environment Variable Examples

Environment variables allow you to configure your n8n instance securely and flexibly. Here's a list of common variables and practical usage examples.

Core Configuration

Variable	Description	Example
N8N_HOST	Hostname for n8n	automation.yourdomain.com
N8N_PORT	Port to run the n8n server on	5678
N8N_PROTOCOL	Protocol used (http/https)	https
N8N_EDITOR_BASE_URL	Public URL for accessing the n8n editor	https://automation.yourdomain.com/
N8N_BASIC_AUTH_ACTIVE	Enables basic auth for editor	true
N8N_BASIC_AUTH_USER	Editor login username	admin

N8N_BASIC_AUTH_PASS WORD	Editor login password	supersecure123

Security & Credentials

Variable	Description	Example
N8N_ENCRYPTION_KEY	Key to encrypt credentials in DB	6B#Df83...
N8N_JWT_SECRET	Secret used for internal auth (multi-user)	secretvalue123
N8N_PERSONALIZATION_ ENABLED	Enable/disable telemetry	false

Database Config

Variable	Description	Example
DB_TYPE	Database type	postgresdb / sqlite
DB_POSTGRESDB_HOST	Host for PostgreSQL	localhost
DB_POSTGRESDB_PORT	Port number	5432

DB_POSTGRESDB_DATA BASE	Database name	n8n_data
DB_POSTGRESDB_USER	Username	n8n_user
DB_POSTGRESDB_PASSW ORD	Password	password123

Email Notifications (Optional)

Variable	Description	Example
N8N_SMTP_HOST	SMTP server host	smtp.gmail.com
N8N_SMTP_PORT	SMTP port	465
N8N_SMTP_USER	SMTP username	user@gmail.com
N8N_SMTP_PASS	SMTP password	app-password

Usage in Docker:

environment:

```
- N8N_BASIC_AUTH_ACTIVE=true

- N8N_BASIC_AUTH_USER=admin

- N8N_BASIC_AUTH_PASSWORD=securepass
```

Appendix D: Full List of 350+ Integrations (By Category)

Below is a categorized breakdown of integrations available in n8n as of the latest release. This list is continually expanding.

Communication Tools

- Gmail, Outlook, SMTP
- Slack, Discord, Microsoft Teams
- Telegram, Twilio, WhatsApp (via Twilio)
- Zoom, SendGrid, Mailgun

Productivity & Collaboration

- Google Calendar, Outlook Calendar
- Notion, Trello, Asana, ClickUp
- Evernote, Todoist, Microsoft OneNote
- Miro, Google Keep

CRM & Marketing

- HubSpot, Salesforce, Pipedrive, Zoho CRM
- ActiveCampaign, Mailchimp, GetResponse
- Intercom, Freshdesk, Zendesk
- Sendinblue, Moosend

E-commerce

- Shopify, WooCommerce, BigCommerce
- Stripe, PayPal, Square
- Amazon Seller Central (via API)
- Shippo, Easyship

Data & Analytics

- Google Sheets, Airtable, Excel Online
- MySQL, PostgreSQL, MongoDB, Redis
- InfluxDB, Google BigQuery
- Redshift, Supabase, Firebase

Web & APIs

- HTTP Request, GraphQL, SOAP
- Webhook (Trigger)
- RSS Feed, Web Scraper
- Puppeteer (headless browser via JS)

AI & Machine Learning

- OpenAI (ChatGPT), Anthropic (Claude)
- Hugging Face, Stability AI
- Google Cloud Vision/NLP
- DeepL, IBM Watson

Developer Tools

- GitHub, GitLab, Bitbucket
- Jira, Linear, ClickUp (dev tasks)
- Docker, Jenkins, CircleCI, Travis CI

File Storage

- Google Drive, Dropbox, OneDrive
- S3, Wasabi, FTP, WebDAV
- Box, Mega

Utility & Core Nodes

- Function, FunctionItem
- Merge, SplitInBatches, Set
- IF, Switch, Wait, Error Trigger
- Cron, DateTime, Environment

Appendix E: Exporting, Importing, and Sharing Workflows

Sharing and reusing workflows in n8n is simple and powerful. This appendix provides a step-by-step guide for exporting, importing, and collaborating with others.

Exporting Workflows

You can export workflows as JSON files. This is useful for version control, backups, or sharing with others.

From the n8n Editor UI:

- Open the workflow you want to export.
- Click the **menu (•••)** in the top right.
- Select **"Export"** → **"Export to File"** or **"Copy to Clipboard"**.
- Save the JSON to a .json file if downloading.

Best Practices:

- Always use meaningful file names (e.g., lead_capture_workflow_v2.json).
- Store exported workflows in Git repositories or cloud folders for collaboration.

Importing Workflows

From JSON File:

- In the n8n editor, click **"New Workflow"**.
- Open the **menu (•••)** and select **"Import from File"**.
- Upload the JSON workflow file.

From Clipboard:

- Copy the workflow JSON.
- Open a new workflow, then select **"Import from Clipboard"**.

Sharing Workflows

Public Sharing via n8n.io

- Visit the n8n community or workflow library.
- You can submit your workflow or find inspiration from existing shared templates.

Via GitHub/GitLab

- Store .json files in repositories with readme docs.
- Great for version tracking and community contributions.

Using the CLI

With n8n export:workflow and n8n import:workflow, you can automate sharing:

```
# Export to file

n8n export:workflow --id=23 --output=workflow23.json
```

Pro Tips:

- Use comments inside node descriptions to explain complex logic.
- Before sharing publicly, remove any credentials or sensitive data.
- Encourage others to fork, clone, or remix workflows for custom use.

Appendix F: Glossary of Automation Terms

This glossary defines key terms and concepts frequently used throughout the book and in the n8n ecosystem.

Term	Definition
Workflow	A series of connected steps (nodes) to automate a task.
Node	An individual task or operation in a workflow (e.g., send email, get data).
Trigger	A node that starts a workflow (e.g., webhook, cron schedule).
Action	A node that performs a task after the trigger (e.g., HTTP request).
Expression	A dynamic formula that pulls or calculates data within a node.

Top 25 Frequently Asked Questions

#	Question	Answer / Solution
1	**Why isn't my workflow triggering?**	Ensure the trigger node is properly configured and the workflow is **active**. For webhooks, confirm the external service is sending data correctly.
2	**How do I test a webhook trigger locally?**	Use tools like **ngrok** to tunnel HTTP requests to your local machine.
3	**What's the difference between 'Execute Workflow' and 'Activate'?**	"Execute Workflow" runs once manually. "Activate" enables the workflow to listen and trigger automatically.
4	**How can I pass data from one node to another?**	Use **expressions** like {{$json["fieldName"]}} to reference data from earlier nodes.
5	**What is the best way to debug a workflow?**	Enable **manual execution**, review **execution logs**, and inspect node outputs and errors.
6	**How do I handle large datasets?**	Use **SplitInBatches**, pagination logic, and avoid

			loading all data into a single node.
7		**Where are credentials stored in n8n?**	In a **secure, encrypted format** within the database or .n8n config depending on deployment.
8		**Can I use environment variables in node fields?**	Yes, reference them with {{$env["VARIABLE_NAME"]}}.
9		**How do I schedule a workflow?**	Use the **Cron node** to trigger workflows on specific intervals or times.
10		**Why is my HTTP Request node failing?**	Check for issues with the API endpoint, headers, method, or missing credentials.
11		**What's the difference between Set and Function nodes?**	**Set** adds or changes static fields, while **Function** allows custom JavaScript logic.
12		**Can I nest workflows or use sub-workflows?**	Yes, using the **Execute Workflow node** to modularize logic.
13		**How can I import a workflow from another project?**	Use the "Import from File" or CLI command: n8n import:workflow.

14	**What does 'No data found' mean in a node?**	Likely the previous node returned no output. Check that data is flowing correctly.
15	**How do I prevent duplicate executions?**	Add conditional checks, use IDs, or add a "Deduplication" logic via expressions or code.
16	**How can I store static configuration data?**	Use the **Static Data** tab or a separate JSON Set node for constants.
17	**How do I make workflows reusable?**	Design modular flows and store templates in a central repository.
18	**Can I use Git with n8n workflows?**	Yes, export workflows as JSON and version control them via Git.
19	**What's the easiest way to clone a node?**	Use the **copy/paste** option or **right-click → Duplicate** in the UI.
20	**Is n8n suitable for production workloads?**	Yes, with proper scaling, error handling, and monitoring (e.g., with Docker or cloud).

21	How can I trigger workflows from other systems?	Via **Webhooks**, **HTTP Requests**, or **Polling** external APIs.
22	Why do I see 'Unknown Error' during execution?	Review the **execution logs**. Often caused by bad expressions, incorrect credentials, or missing fields.
23	How can I retry a failed execution?	Use **retry logic** in error handling or manually re-execute from the execution log.
24	Can I use AI (like ChatGPT) in my workflow?	Yes, via **OpenAI nodes** or custom HTTP requests with APIs like GPT, Claude, etc.
25	What resources are available to learn more?	Official docs, YouTube tutorials, Slack/Discord community, and this book!

Common Troubleshooting Tips

- **Problem**: "Workflow does not activate."
  - **Fix**: Ensure all required credentials are added, and the trigger node is valid.
- **Problem**: "Node returns '401 Unauthorized'."
  - **Fix**: Check API keys, OAuth tokens, or environment variables. Ensure they're correctly referenced.
- **Problem**: "n8n crashes or restarts frequently (self-hosted)."
  - **Fix**: Inspect logs (docker logs, journalctl) and ensure enough memory/CPU is allocated.
- **Problem**: "Webhook URL returns 404."

- **Fix**: Workflow must be activated, and the URL must match the expected endpoint exactly.
- **Problem**: "Node output is empty or undefined."
  - **Fix**: Validate previous node outputs, use the **Debug** tab, and ensure expected data exists.
- **Problem**: "Docker container not saving workflows."
  - **Fix**: Use **volume mounts** for persistent storage: -v ~/.n8n:/home/node/.n8n.
- **Problem**: "Workflow runs repeatedly or loops."
  - **Fix**: Add control logic or checks to prevent self-triggering (e.g., IF or Switch nodes).